Praise for

Capture the Rapt

"This practical, well-written book is filled with all you need to know to build a magical, rapture-filled life."
—CHERYL RICHARDSON
AUTHOR OF *TAKE TIME FOR YOUR LIFE*

"It's one thing to go after the life you've always wanted, but *Capture the Rapture* makes it possible to get there. Don't miss this practical, nurturing labor of love."
—RICHARD BRODIE
AUTHOR OF *GETTING PAST OK* AND *VIRUS OF THE MIND*

"*Rapture* is insightful in an exceptionally easy-to-understand way. *Rapture* is practical in a way all of us can start using today. *Rapture* is inspiring . . . your smile will blossom and your spirit will rise. With Marcia's experienced help, live your life in rapture!"
—RICHARD HAASNOOT
AUTHOR OF *THE NEW WISDOM OF BUSINESS*

"A good life is about vision. This book is about finding your personal vision. *Capture the Rapture* is an unusually valuable resource for anyone who wishes to transform their life."
—WAYNE AND TAMARA MITCHELL
RELATIONSHIP ADVICE COLUMNISTS AND COAUTHORS OF
YOUR OTHER HALF

Capture the Rapture

Capture the Rapture

How to Step Out of Your Head and Leap into Life

Marcia Reynolds

Hathor Hill Press
Scottsdale, Arizona

Published by:
Hathor Hill Press
PO Box 5012
Scottsdale, AZ 85261

Editor: Ellen Kleiner
Book design and production: Janice St. Marie
Cover art and design: Ellen E. Abbott
Back cover photo: John Hall

Printed in the United States of America on acid-free recycled paper

Publisher's Cataloging-in-Publication Data

Reynolds, Marcia.
    Capture the rapture : how to step out of your
    head and leap into life / Marcia Reynolds. — 1st
    ed.
        p. cm.
        Includes bibliographic references.
        LCCN: 99-97659
        ISBN: 0-9655250-0-7

        1. Self-actualization (Psychology).
    2. Interpersonal relationships. 3. Job satisfaction.
    I. Title.

BF637.S4R49 2000   158
                  QBI00-74

For Debbie
Who teaches me, daily,
what unconditional love is all about.

For Carol
Who pushes me over the edge into
the true joy of my experience.

For PK
Who shows me that living like a princess
is a deliciously dignified way to be.

Acknowledgments

It has been twenty-five years since Vicki, my cellmate and soulmate, told me, "The next time I see your name, it will be in print." I can only hope she is still alive, and that somehow this book will find its way to her.

The road has been long. I'm most grateful to my best friend Debbie, who found me again when I was in college, struggling to make it on my own, and who brought me back to my writing. She lovingly edits my crude first drafts, talks me through my blocks, and tells me the truth when I need to hear it. She is the Betty to my Bobby Brown (with credit to Kurt Vonnegut for these characters). Without her, my cup would be half empty.

Along the road, I've met so many wonderful people. I'd especially like to name those who make me smile. First and foremost is Paul Jantzi, who fills me with enough joy to last an eternity. Then there's the sisterhood—Wendy White, Paulette Pohlmann, Linda Lunden, Vicki Sullivan, Alice Adams-Sax, Agnes Mura, DJ Mitsch, Toni Koch—my sister Eve, my niece Jennie, and the scores of beautiful angels who fly through my life. Whenever I'm down, Michael Harris and Bob Benkendorf appear to remind me that we're on this planet to be happy. And special acknowledgment goes to my partner, guide, playmate, and friend, Gary Mason, for brightening my days with mountains, flowers, and hot fudge sundaes.

The birth of this book is due to the gifts and wisdom of Ellen Kleiner, my editor and book producer, who held to her high standards, ensuring we had a manuscript worthy of publication. Ellen always knew what I wanted to say, and that what I had to say was important. She is a tolerant and graceful midwife.

Finally, I thank my mother for laughing so hard, she'd cry, and my father for teaching me how to leap.

Contents

Preface

Two weeks after I left my corporate position, I interrupted my writing period to dash to the mailbox. On my return, I stopped at the garden to smell a cluster of American Beauties. I laughed at how delightful it felt to have my life resemble a cliché. Then a sadness washed over me. I had lived in my house for five years, yet could not recall the last time I'd inhaled the roses' sweet fragrance. To cope with a stressful job, I had turned off my senses. I'd dulled myself to life.

Back at my desk, I set pen to paper. How much of my life was I living on "automatic pilot"? I had to know the answer. I recorded what I could remember of how I had spent the previous three months. When I stopped to read the words, I found entire pages filled with reports of routines and tasks, with few references to how I felt about them. Where feelings did appear, their descriptions were brief and trite. I could see that although my life now ranked lower on the stress scale, it lacked heart.

This realization launched me on a quest for happiness. I bought books on how to tune in to inner truth. I listened to tapes on how to release the child within. I attended seminars on how to clear out garbage from the past and clutter from the present to create a more vibrant future. I went dancing, tracked down old friends, and read the novels stacked on my nightstand. At times, I felt entertained and enlightened. Mostly, I felt exhausted.

Unable to experience exuberance in my hometown of Phoenix, Arizona, I turned to the wilderness, thinking the wind might whisper ancient wisdom to me on a quiet night far from city lights. I bought a twenty-four-foot camper-trailer and, with my best friend Debbie, took off for Montana. We walked in the shadow of Indian totems and sandstone hoodoos. We glimpsed grizzly bears, moose, and buffalo. We gazed in awe at clear crater lakes and majestic sculptured canyons. Our fellow RV-campers were friendly and fun; the store clerks, curious and helpful. But, although grateful to be in the natural world, I felt like a spectator. While appreciating the beauty, I could not feel it in my bones.

On the last leg of our return journey, we camped at Priest Gulch, near Rico, Colorado. While hiking along the nearby creek one afternoon, I started to cry. The muscles in my chest cramped up. I couldn't breathe. My legs crumbled. Falling to my knees, I screamed, "Where is my passion?"

The words bounced off granite walls and slid down the trail toward the creek. Leaning against a large rock, I hugged my knees to my chest and wailed, "Where did my enthusiasm go?" I tried to remember the last time I had attacked a project with zeal. Flashbacks to my college years and my first job reminded me of times my heart had been consumed by fire. Anguish, exhilaration, outrage, pride, and other powerful emotions had surged through my body. Are such sensations indigenous to youth alone, I wondered, or have layers of disappointment doused the flame? Are my feelings gone or simply dormant? "Please, God, help me find them," I cried. "I'm dead and I want to live."

Leaves rustled overhead, yet I heard no answers. My feet carried my heavy body back to camp.

As it turned out, my prayer had reached its mark. After returning home, I began to focus my research not only on how to find happiness but also on how to revive passion. Weaving these themes into my work, I began to contract with companies interested in having me teach communication skills to their employees. Six months later my first audiotape program, on how to be powerfully present, hit bookstore shelves. Many people who had purchased the tape called to have me coach them through complacency, frustration, and disillusionment. In the guidance I gave them were answers to the questions I had posed on that mountain trail in Colorado.

Central to them all was an emerging understanding that there is a huge difference between "existing" and "living." The practices I'd learned from the books and tapes had me existing—learning to be content with present circumstances and to settle into a little cradle of life that was peaceful, secure ... and stifling. The comfort zone, I realized, is a respite from life, not a way to participate in it. As social activist and poet Naomi Littlebear says, "Complacency is a more dangerous emotion than outrage." Either you create a vision and act on it, or you suffer the frustration of standing still.

Indeed, some of the most profound testimonials of joy come from the poor, the sick, champion athletes, adventurers, and children. Most people leading "normal" lives, on the other hand, muddle through their days compiling long lists of regrets to summarize on their deathbeds. They stare at walls in waiting rooms, watch clocks at the office, and sleepwalk their way through endless chores at home. Their smiles are induced by alcohol, memories of past experiences, or silly banter on television. Even as they accept awards and sign contracts to purchase luxury homes, their laughter sounds more like sighs. They measure success by their bank statements.

"When I got to this destination called 'success,'" says Ladies Professional Golf Association hall of famer Carol Mann, "it wasn't what I thought it should be. It was transitory. I got bored and wasn't gratified on the inside." Today, Mann focuses on designing golf courses and teaching women's and junior golf programs. Her pleasure is in the execution, not the outcome. "I didn't get these kinds of stimulations on tour," she adds. "Now I live in fertile ground."

"Existing" lacks enjoyment; "living" brims over with enchantment. When you are living, anything—the air you breathe, the sun's warmth, a penny on the sidewalk—can trigger a smile and send a warm glow through your veins. Living fully is to realize your potential, to be aware of who you are and all that is around you in each waking moment. To get there, you need to *step out of your head and leap into life*.

The sojourn from barren days to moments of bliss is no easy trek. You have to bust the dam across your emotional river. Unfortunately, while we humans work to increase our material gain, we do little to enhance our experience of joy. To see this regrettable law of existence in action, next time you are waiting to board an airplane, try to identify travelers who are on vacation by looking at their facial expressions, rather than their clothing. You are likely to find that those on their way to Hawaii look as unexcited as folks flying to Omaha for business. In a sense, most of our lives are spent waiting for something. We save money to go to school; we go to school to get a good job; we work so that we can retire; then we proceed with caution so as to live longer. My mother, who all her life repressed her desires, asked to be cremated so that her money would not be spent frivolously. If she were here now, I'd take her dancing.

The pursuit of happiness is so important that Thomas Jefferson named it one of our three inalienable rights in the Declaration of Independence. However, the quest itself often leads to disappointment. The leisure industry is exploding. Comedies top the Nielsen ratings. Yet both chemical and herbal antidepressants are consumed like candy. And when asked, "What did you do last weekend?" few people can remember by Monday afternoon. Among those who can, the words "I felt happy" rarely show up in their reply.

Joy is a way of being, not doing. And learning to *be* takes courage, perseverance, and trust. Those who tackle the challenge come to meet and love their true selves. As a result, they experience "being their joy." In the words of world-renowned mythologist Joseph Campbell, "One of the greatest of life's privileges is to be who you are."

Do you want to wake up each morning grateful for being alive? Would you like your heart to fill with an energy so vibrant that it flows to your eyes, fingers, and toes? Wouldn't it be awesome to act freely, assured that you have the power to "be" anything? In truth, this power belongs to us all and no one can take it away from us. May you learn, as I did, to step out of thinking and planning and waiting and doing to finally enjoy the pleasure of being.

Introduction

Many people say they love the idea of a passionate and joyful life, but doubt they will have one this time around. They long to immerse themselves in happiness, yet count their blessings if a day goes by free of crisis. Hearing such statements, one cannot help but wonder if these individuals have given up on the journey before setting sail. Worse, many top professionals in our medical and scientific communities support such complacency.

A new premise, dubbed the "happiness set-point theory," purports to explain why some people bounce back after difficulties whereas others stay sad or angry for months. The theory proposes that what determines how happy we will be is genetics, not external events or self-awareness. Dr. David Lykken, who has been investigating the physiology of happiness based on his studies of twins, estimates that 80 percent of our sense of well-being is determined by a "hardwired" baseline established at conception. Recent brain-imaging research supports Dr. Lykken's conclusions. It reveals that children who show positive emotion year after year have more activity in the left prefrontal areas of the brain than children who are temperamentally low key, pessimistic, or angry.

These findings give us good reason to stop comparing ourselves with people who deliriously spring out of bed each morning and bound up two mountains before breakfast. Still, must we blame our murky existence on genes? Although the theory may hold substance, it seems we humans have the capacity to build on the wits we were born with. Those of us who have struggled with set-points of weight—who have hit a wall in weight loss that is hard to break through—know that a good diet and daily exercise will eventually lower the set-point. Likewise, couldn't a good mental diet and regular exercise in self-awareness elevate the set-point of happiness? When altering our weight, we may be lucky to drop two pounds a week. When altering our outlook, we may add only two smiles a day. Even so, it is our birthright as human beings to go for the change.

Psychologist Abraham Maslow, celebrated pioneer of the self-actualization model, believed in each person's ability to reach out and create the world of their dreams. His research, too, suggests that individuals have the innate ability to go beyond their perceived capacities. In essence, he showed that anyone can rise to a higher level of self-actualizing once they are able to stop worrying about survival. Maslow's work substantially contradicts the findings of set-point theorists.

Certainly, transcending a set-point takes hard work. The mind needs to think new thoughts—otherwise, all we are doing is recycling old familiar ones. The practice also requires bravery. Passionate joy is similar to true love which, according to psychologist Nathaniel Brandon, "requires courage—the courage to stay vulnerable, to stay open to our feelings ... even when we are frustrated, hurt, angry—the courage to stay open rather than shut down emotionally, even when it is terribly tempting to do so." Above all, moving to new levels of happiness calls for *faith*. If you feel trapped, overwhelmed, and unable to believe you can live a joyful life, you won't. Yet if you see life as a veritable bowl of pleasures, you will be able to eat its fruits. If you know that on the other side of disappointment lies a better opportunity, you will touch rainbows. If you trust that there are forces at work to help you transcend a ground-zero existence, you will fly.

A leap of faith is sometimes confusing, and at other times painful. It offers no guarantees of wealth or soulmates. It demands a firm commitment in terms of time, tears, and openheartedness. Yet if you are willing to take this leap, a great wonderment awaits you. Regardless of your circumstances, you can access the power to live to your fullest potential physically, emotionally, and spiritually. In Zimbabwe, it is said, "If you can walk, you can dance. If you can talk, you can sing." Likewise, if you can breathe, you can be whimsical, playful, adventurous, and serene all at once—harmonizing with the world around you. In fact, you have the capacity to create a life of passionate joy *right now*, if you wish. Beginning today, you can facilitate change, experience deeper levels of love, speak your truth, and follow your dreams.

This guidebook has been designed to help you take flight. Each chapter blends strategies, exercises, and games with illuminating anecdotes and examples to spark your creative energy and prompt you to release your passion. In the vein of *The Joy of Cooking* and *The Joy of Sex*, it provides recipes for the joy of living.

Part I lays the groundwork, fortifying you for the adventure. First, you will shore up your foundation by claiming your greatness and filling the cracks that erode your confidence. Then you will begin to build resilience for weathering the crises, disappointments, and losses that invariably arise.

Part II presents a map for entering "the zone" that leads to the kingdom of the present moment. Here you will master four milestones: declaring your purpose, constructing your vision, bridging the gap between your vision and current circumstances, and maximizing your energy as you move ever more consciously into new present moments. Since most people you associate with will continue to structure their lives by time and expectation, you are likely to encounter frustration; if you do, understand that there is greater joy to be found by faithfully following your map. From time to time, you will be revisiting the four landmarks, only to find them evolving, as you are.

Part III, the final portion of this book, explores how to seize your passion in specific settings—at work, at play, and in love. It goes on to demonstrate ways to cultivate seeds of gratitude, abundance, and laughter for further nourishment. Loving life, you will find, does not squelch feelings of desire or pain. Instead, it enlarges your field of perception, enabling you to take in a wide-angle view of the many emotional textures that dwell in each precious present.

The techniques and exercises described in these pages, although proven successful, are intended as navigational guidelines only, not solid rules. Adapt them to your personal style. Take your time. Prepare for fluctuations in the ups and downs, gains and losses, understanding and discouragement that surface from one day to the next. Above all, open continually to the possibility of enhanced self-discovery, self-expression, and happiness. If receiving these gifts at first feels selfish, remember that the experience of joy is your ultimate contribution to the universe. Not only will you serve as a beacon, showing others what is possible, but exhilaration is the finest way of saying "thank you" for the opportunity to live on this glorious planet.

Unfortunately, this book cannot lead you to perpetual bliss. It will, however, help you feel the power of passion's energy. Surely, this must be what the Sufi poet Rumi was referring to when he wrote, "The most important thing in life is to become a passionate lover. If you've not been a passionate lover of life, then count not your life as having been lived."

May you find in these pages everything you need to construct your wings and ride the currents of passion. Use the first two chapters while preparing for takeoff. The remaining chapters are your flying lessons.

Part I

THE PLEASURE
OF BEING

*Living in a fog,
you forget how sunshine feels.*

—Peter D. Kramer

Many people readily admit that they are searching for meaning, purpose, and deeper levels of happiness. Some turn to religion or spirituality. Others voraciously devour seminars, books, and audio-tapes. Still others go to movies exploring the meaning of life, death, and whatever might lie beyond. Yet, although all these individuals keep very busy "doing things," they are still disappointed and frustrated. Some may be fortunate enough to find a level of contentment. The rest fall into a pit of lethargy. They acknowledge that "something is missing" but cannot say what it is. They lose their zest for living. The problem is that they are searching in the "horizontal world."

Americans, as well as an increasing portion of Westernized populations, live in the horizontal world. We move from one activity to the next, all the while feeling angst about the past and fearful of the future.

Even meditation is carved into our schedules as an "appointment" to keep with ourselves. While moving across the horizontal plane of existence, those of us who stop to pay attention tend to analyze what we pick up on, label it good or bad, then react. Our minds ring with judgment. We search endlessly for answers, seeking to control whatever brings us love, entertainment, and freedom from pain. Whether we trudge or skip through agendas, the movement is usually from one destination to the next, from one goal, one desire, or one promise to another . . . until illness or crisis intervenes, signaling the need for a break.

Five years ago, my personal coach suggested that to find happiness I spend one full day doing nothing—no reading, no watching TV, no housecleaning, or even solitaire. From the moment I woke up, I was edgy. Unable to silence my mind with familiar distractions, I finally took myself to a park, where anxiety tortured me for hours. Eventually, I began to notice the beauty of the trees, the grace of the springtime weather, and the delight of the people who wandered through the nearby playground.

That flash of awareness marked my first conscious step into the "vertical world"—the sphere of life composed only of what we can touch, taste, smell, see, and hear, and what we can feel in our hearts. In the vertical world, we operate with clear intentions, knowing who we are and what we are doing. Here the mind, free of chatter, acts as a receptacle for possibilities and the body spontaneously responds. We may stumble or fall. Yet after a good laugh or cry, we dust ourselves off and carry on. We have no attachment to details. We are free of preoccupations. Like children, we see the world with innocent eyes, playing in the glorious here and now.

While sitting in the park, I caught only glimpses into this world. I was merely sightseeing and, like a tourist, I could not appreciate what it was like to reside there. In fact, after a few hours spent leaning against a tree, I fell asleep. A barking dog roused me. I went home feeling numb.

Not long after, at the urging of an actress friend I signed up to attend an improvisation camp put on by Artistic New Directions in New York's Catskill Mountains. My goal was to add drama and comedy to my public-speaking routines, to enhance my performances with authenticity. I went to improvisation camp to increase my impact on the stage. I left with a new perspective on life.

The first improvisation session was led by Carol Fox Prescott, an acting coach based in New York City. Carol coached us to "seek the joy" of our experience. Until an actor can reach the moment of uninhibited expression, we were told, her action is an impersonation, something not fully alive. To reach the peak of performance, the transition from "doing" to "being," one must release all emotion—let loose a hearty laugh, allow for a good cry, dance to sweet music, belt out a favorite song, sensuously love, ardently hate, scream with delight or anguish. Carol challenged me to face my limits, then pushed me over the edge. Embarrassment was never reason enough to stop. She modeled, coddled, coaxed, and commanded, making me repeat the same lines over and over until passion broke through, overpowering my fear.

While working with Carol, I realized that to improve on stage you must come to know your hopes, fears, strengths, and needs—not as good or bad, but as the elements that make up the glorious person you are. Aware of your inner experience, you begin to acknowledge the twist in your stomach when you feel pushed, the skip of your heart when you are called on to speak, the hole in your chest when your heart breaks, the rush in your veins when you have been touched by a lover. You feel all this energy and then you release it while exhaling, touching, speaking, and moving.

Such self-awareness is not self-consciousness. With self-awareness your emotions, rather than stifling your experience of life, flow through you as you interact with the world. Your mind, instead of analyzing and making decisions, rides those waves of emotion and thereby avoids being sucked in by the undertow. Your emotions then become *sources of information* to use in understanding life's lessons and in sorting out the maze of subtle nuances that color your relationships.

As a result of Carol's coaching, I basked in the vertical world. I learned how to capture the ecstasy of moments both on stage and off. Since then, I have been exploring ways to *live* in this vertical world, ways to embrace the pleasure of being. I have also been attempting to untangle the paradox that although we humans most desire to be known and loved, we struggle with our vulnerability.

I found that entry into the vertical world's pleasure of being hinges on two steps. The first is to build a strong personal foundation based on self-awareness and confidence, a subject addressed in chapter 1.

The stronger our foundation is, the better able we are to demolish the walls that have imprisoned our passion. Before long, we discover that living life fully is easier than struggling, fighting, or hiding from it.

The second step into the pleasure of being is to cultivate tools for climbing out of the ruts left in the wake of hard times. Proficiency in the use of these resiliency tools, which are described in chapter 2, comes with practice. Opportunities for practice arise in the common annoyances we face every day.

Armed with a strong foundation and strategies for coping with crisis, you can take the leap into being. For at that point you will know that no matter what happens—no matter how high you fly or how hot it gets—your wings will never melt.

CHAPTER 1

Strengthening Your Foundation

*Skills and confidence
are an unconquerable army.*

—George Herbert

When I was a child, my parents told me I could do anything, which was a great gift. Then they added, "You're better than everyone else," which was a great responsibility.

I trotted off to elementary school feeling all-powerful. Reality hit the first day. I met Lindy Allison, my first blonde. No matter how adorably I smiled and blushed, the boys liked Lindy better. I was cute. Lindy was cuter.

Then we had our first spelling test. I missed one word. Deborah Basehore missed none. Throughout the years, I earned straight A's. I was the smartest person in class, almost. Deborah was smarter.

I still had my father to please, so I set out to find what I could do better than everyone else. Modeling my dad, I told jokes and acted silly, stealing the stage from my teachers. The kids laughed more at me than at anyone else. If a teacher punished me, I spoke my mind before obeying. My classmates cheered me on. Sometimes I had to sit at my desk while everyone else went out for recess. When I felt lonely, I consoled myself by writing funny plays for my schoolmates to act in. They applauded my work. Students in every grade knew my name. I became the most popular kid in class, giving my father something to boast about.

Life was grand ... until I turned fourteen. Then, in August 1969, my parents transported me to a new world called high school. Traits and activities held in esteem in grade school were labeled square at West High. I struggled to stand out in the sea of new faces, to talk hip and cope with the sexual pressures. Since most of the kids had turned their focus from academics and sports to drugs, I strove to maintain my popularity by proving that I could do drugs better than everyone else. LSD, marijuana, methamphetamine, barbiturates...I did drugs so well that two years after I graduated, I earned an all-expense-paid six-month vacation in the county jail.

After that, life spiraled downward. To this day, scars mark my arms, bringing up memories of missed opportunities, damaged friendships, shameful sex, close calls with losing my life, watching others lose theirs, and the anguish my parents fought so hard to bear. In another sense, going to jail was the best thing that happened to me.

I limped into my cell, a scared, gawky, sickly nineteen-year-old heroin addict. My thin jail-issued blanket offered me refuge during the first few days. Then, after my body had weaned itself off the drug, my cellmates deemed me strong enough to withstand their ridicule. They made fun of my every move, calling me "white punk" and "pecker popper," and other, more descriptive names.

I bore the brunt of their attacks for about a week. At that point, tired of the humiliation and loneliness, I reached into my past for solutions. I told jokes, made fun of the female guards, and acted so outrageously my tormentors could not help but laugh. In jail, laughter soothes the heart. If a guard scolded me, I spoke my mind. I occasionally ended up in isolation, earning a hero's reputation. While in isolation, I wrote poetry for the women to send to their husbands, lovers, and children. My elementary-school tactics soon won me many friends, including Vicki.

Vicki, leader of the biggest and meanest gang, had managed to procure me as her cellmate. If you've never been confined to a jail cell, imagine for a moment that you live in a bathroom—one with only a toilet and sink. Now add just enough space for two or four bunk beds and three to seven people of your own gender. You all sleep, eat, excrete, secrete, laugh, scream, and cry together in this tiny cubicle. Twice a day you are released to take a shower and watch television for about two hours—that is, you are released if the house isn't over-crowded. If it is, you have to stay in the "bathroom" for an indeterminate number of days until conditions change. Should you get angry, you risk losing visits with your family, plus your mail, candy bars, and cigarettes. All that is left is stale air, dirty walls, sweaty bodies, and the same sad faces day in and day out.

One particularly warm Sunday, Vicki, our two cellmates, and I were informed that the vice squad had raided Van Buren Street, mean-ing our cellblock was brimming with prostitutes. Because of the over-crowding, we would be on lockup for at least a week. This marked the third such restriction that month. To make matters worse, we knew that a larger cellblock on the floor was empty, since its residents—all men—had recently been transferred to another jail. But moving us over was an administrative hassle. Our comfort was not a priority.

When we heard about the lockup, Vicki exploded. "I'm gonna hurt someone," she said.

At that point, Vicki and I were several months into our friendship. My boldness had caught her eye. My card-playing competence won her respect. My humor and creativity eased her wrath. I, in turn, loved her brashness, her pluck, and her willingness to act in fiery defense of "her women." Yet it hurt me to watch her constantly battling with Lieutenant Davis, reigning officer of the women guards. Vicki usually lost. In those moments, tears dissolved her tough exterior and a con-fused, abused, lonely little girl showed through.

Coming from a culture that expounded, "Make love not war," I offered Vicki an alternative to hurting someone. "How about a group protest," I suggested. "Nonviolent, like Gandhi."

"Gandhi shot," Vicki replied.

I ignored her. "Like Martin Luther King."

"King shot, too."

I glared at her. "Do you want to do something about this or not?"

She looked at me sideways. "Like what?"

I came up with a plan for staging a protest and shared it with her.

She liked it. Calling the idea out into the catwalk, she rallied support from her gang, who proceeded to inform the other inmates. To our surprise, the entire cellblock vocalized their approval.

I yelled the instructions. Then cell by cell I checked to make sure everyone understood. They declared their readiness.

We began with silence. Each cough and bed squeak echoed loudly, like sounds in a music hall before the orchestra's first note.

When we heard keys unlocking the catwalk door, Vicki started to kick the wall. I accompanied her. Within seconds, the entire cellblock was rocking to the beat.

A female guard yelled, "Stop it! What's going on?"

The kicking intensified.

I chanted, "Captain, captain," and the others joined in the chorus.

The guard ran out.

Lieutenant Davis entered the catwalk. "Stop this *now!*" she barked.

We chanted, "Captain, captain."

She stormed out.

The pounding started to die. "*Don't* stop now!" I yelled.

The beat picked up again. Just when it felt as though my legs would fall off, the door opened once more.

This time a loud male voice boomed down the walk, "Girls!"

I winced at the word.

"Quiet. Now. Or there'll be trouble."

The noise died down. The captain, flanked by the guard and Lieutenant Davis, marched to our cell. "All right, Vicki," he said. "What's going on?"

I sat up. "Why 'Vicki'? *She* didn't start it."

He looked at Lieutenant Davis. "Who's this?"

Vicki jumped up. "Why are we on restriction? Why can't we shower?"

"We want answers," I insisted.

The captain cleared his throat. "We have good reason."

"Bullshit," Vicki said.

The other inmates hollered in consent.

Speaking loud enough for everyone to hear, the captain said, "You're out of line. That's full restriction for three days. Straighten up or I'll make it a week."

I winked at Vicki. She yelled, "Garbage!"

We all threw our trash into the catwalk. When our cell's garbage pail was empty, Vicki hurled it against the bars.

The captain called out, "I mean it!"

I yelled, "Dresses!" We ripped off our dresses and threw them into the catwalk. Hundreds of buttons tapped the cement like rain on a tin roof.

"That's it!" The captain stormed out, his entourage trailing behind him.

Soon our cell door opened. Five male guards rushed in and grabbed Vicki. She fought back.

I heard the words "stupid bitch" and saw one of the guards reach for the stick on his belt. It slid upward—

"No!" The word sprang out of my mouth. I leaped like a cat, claws and teeth bared, pushing, scratching, biting. My head met steel. My jaw snapped. A fist landed in my stomach as large hands squeezed my wrists and pinned them behind me. The men dragged Vicki and me out of our cell, through the main door, then down another hall to an isolation cell.

They dropped Vicki first, and me on top of her. Pushing me away, she sprang to her feet and stumbled toward the door, but it slammed before she could reach it. She kicked the steel slab, then crumbled to the floor.

I sniffed, and gargled mucus. Wiping my nose and mouth, I noticed streaks of blood on the back of my hand. I rubbed them off on my torn underwear. Yellow and purple patches dotted my legs. I dropped my chin.

"Sorry. I'm so stupid," I mumbled. "Nothing I do works out. My life is one big dumb failure."

I heard her body creak as she rose up and shuffled toward me. Next thing I knew, she had smashed her open hand into my chest.

"Stop it," she snarled.

I gasped, my voice splintering under the force of her thrust.

She leaned her face into mine. "You are *not* a loser," she said. "You're smart. You're strong." She stopped bearing down, but her hand still pressed against my skin. "And for some reason known only to God, you care about people. When you get that in *there*," she said, pushing against my heart, "you'll get out of *here*." She pointed to the door.

There was nothing to say. All I could do was memorize her words so that they would stay with me.

The next day, several guards moved all the women but us to the larger cellblock. Vicki and I were escorted to one where they kept inmates who were required to be separated from the general population. We never saw the other women again. I was released two months later.

Vicki's words did stay with me. In fact, I committed them to paper so that I could keep them in my pocket as well as in my heart. While facing the possibility of doing drugs again, I remembered them: "You're smart. You're strong. You care." Staying clean was hard, but I did it. Upon entering college, I remembered them. Three years later, I graduated summa cum laude and left Phoenix for the first time ever to attend graduate school. To overcome my fear of failure, I remembered them. I then returned to Phoenix, where I was offered a job as a corporate trainer. The first time I stood in front of a group, I remembered them: "You're smart. You're strong. You care." I kept that list of what made me special and added to it year after year, each time further strengthening the foundation of who I knew myself to be.

Today, armed with two master's degrees and nearly two decades of corporate work, I run a successful business providing seminars and personal coaching to help people be their best. I have each of my clients make a list of their personal powers to carry with them through difficult times. "It's a gift," I tell them. "One that I received from an angel named Vicki."

While on this adventure called life, you too can develop confidence, strengthening the foundation that holds you aloft in the world. Once fortified, this bedrock will allow you to lift off and embrace the pleasure of being. The initial reinforcement comes from laying claim to your personal powers, evaporating your fears, recognizing your needs, and taking extremely good care of yourself.

CLAIMING YOUR PERSONAL POWERS

Doing things well assists us in achieving our goals. Yet being all of who we are takes us much further, for it calls on such personal powers as confidence, compassion, conviction, and love. Whereas my father helped me realize all that I could *do* in life, Vicki showed me all that I could *be*. "Doing" earns us praise. "Being" brings us joy.

The awareness of who we are ushers us beyond an *understanding* of existence to an *experience* of it. Given the chance to experience who we are, we become empowered to persevere and manifest our dreams. Knowing "who I can be" in addition to "what I can do" unshackles the spirit. As Franklin Delano Roosevelt said, "I choose not to be a common man. It's my right to be uncommon. . . . I want to take the calculated risk to dream and to build, to fail and to succeed. I refuse to live from hand to mouth. I prefer the challenge of life to the guaranteed existence. The thrill of fulfillment to the still calm of utopia. I will never cower to any master, nor bend to any threat. It's my heritage to stand erect; proud and unafraid to face the world." Roosevelt chose to "be" uncommon and courageous—strengths that lifted the country out of depression and into prosperity.

Who you are may not be who you think you are. For instance, who you are is not what you say when you introduce yourself at a party. Saying, "I'm a lawyer (a Democrat, a mother of four, a single parent, a Catholic, a baby boomer, an animal lover)," identifies a group you claim allegiance to. These are roles you play. Although they dictate certain behavior, you can always change the rules, the titles, and the protocols. So do not mistake these labels for the real you; in fact, the energy spent defending them may only weaken your ability to reach your highest potential. You are not what you do or the groups you belong to. You are the *sum of your personal powers*—your abilities to create.

To claim your personal powers, you will first need to uncover them. Once you find them and come to know them intimately, you must then shout them out to the world and speak of them unashamedly with your family, friends, and colleagues. In doing so, you will liberate your capacity to manifest all that you desire and, in the process, transform the world around you.

Self-Discovery through a Personal Power Inventory

One of the simplest ways to uncover your strengths is by conducting a personal power inventory. Added together, the items you arrive at will reveal the power you have to shape your future. Power, in this context, refers to strengths that cannot be taken away. Money, credentials, and possessions do not qualify, for they can disappear in a day. Nor do classic good looks count, since they can easily succumb to the ravages of aging, injury, or illness. In fact, mastering the fear of aging is a far greater triumph than using technology to stay one step ahead of nature. Even your skills—how well you speak, hunt, cook, handle finances, play sports, see the "big picture," negotiate, mediate, teach, or write—can be lost to time or stolen by circumstance.

The power involved in shaping a future is perhaps best defined by Tracy Goss, author of *The Last Word on Power*, who wrote, "Power to make something impossible happen is a very sophisticated form of power. It is completely different from the forms of power that most people, even successful people, have learned during the course of their lives. It bears no relation to authority. ... It has nothing to do with competence. ... And it does not require influence. ... When you acquire this power, you can operate with a quality and integrity that frees you to take the risks and actions necessary to change the world."

During a vacation in Malaysia, I was confined to my room for a few hours each morning while it rained. I passed the time reading a stack of *Success* magazines thoughtfully furnished by the resort. Each issue featured at least two stories about people overcoming great odds to realize their dreams. Every one of these heroes, as it turned out, credited their unexpected accomplishments to a *variety* of factors. Similarly, in conducting your personal power inventory you will be looking for a composite of attributes. No single characteristic ensures victory; talented people lose, courageous people fall, and smart people fail. Rather, it is the *sum* of the elements that determines the magnitude of your power.

The personal power inventory is a tool that encourages you to itemize three forms of power: knowledge power (KP), relationship power (RP), and inner power (IP). Added together, your knowledge power, your relationship power, and your inner power will equal your personal power (PP), as is illustrated below.

Personal Power Inventory

$$KP + RP + IP = PP$$

Knowledge Power (KP). This is the easiest form of power to attain. Although education contributes strongly to the KP category, while conducting your inventory remember that wisdom comes through many channels. As Alan Weiss, author of *The Million Dollar Consultant*, writes, "A high IQ score has no bearing on one's actual applied intelligence or success in life. All it demonstrates is a high test score." Every day holds the potential for fresh insight and bits of information that may prove helpful in the future. Even painful experiences offer valuable lessons that lead to growth. To regret such an experience is to miss the lesson. To learn from it is to develop a personal strength.

Knowledge power also encompasses an experience of your daily surroundings, rich as they are with information. Novels in addition to newspapers broaden your perspective. Creative thinking and innovative risk-taking allow you to see "beyond the box." Intuition and inventive decision-making hold more weight than the faint memory of a college curriculum. Include on your list of knowledge powers your attentiveness, degree of open-mindedness, and willingness to learn. For a sample listing of knowledge powers, together with the other powers, see page 34.

Relationship Power (RP). Relationship strengths are becoming increasingly important in every sphere of life, especially the business world. Lean companies dependent on teamwork for results can no longer afford to downplay the significance of listening skills and sensitivity. The need for a kinder, gentler working environment is not a fad; it's a bottom-line necessity.

Likewise, communities, families, and partnerships of all sorts demand enhanced communication skills. Societies around the world have witnessed major shifts in husband-wife, parent-child, boyfriend-girlfriend, manager-employee, and doctor-patient roles. Whereas people entering these relationships once had a preconceived idea of how to act and what to expect, such clarity no longer exists. With this in mind, include on your list of relationship powers the desire to listen; the ability to hear emotion as well as content; the willingness to understand, articulate, and use emotions as information; and the capacity to offer empathy, compassion, positive energy, and respect.

Inner Power (IP). This form of power, although the most important of them all, is the most difficult to describe. Religious literature often portrays these strengths as the presence of calm and the ability to love all living creatures. Other inner powers are the capacity to receive love, excitement about being alive, and the drive to fight for personal truths. Love, coupled with the courage and commitment to stand up for one's beliefs, provides a foundation for other strengths. If devotion is the focus of your daily activities, you will feel in control of your life. And if your dauntless dedication touches others and stirs their hearts, you just may be able to change the world. Fun, too, is an inner power, since lightness, mirth, and a frisky nature attract life's greatest riches. Therefore, include on your list of inner powers such traits as enthusiasm, determination, devotion, love of self, love of others, love of life, unity with a higher power, faith, peacefulness, a sense of humor, playfulness, and the ability to "go with the flow."

How to Conduct a Personal Power Inventory

Your inventory will consist of three lists—one for KP, one for RP, and one for IP. To begin, record the personal power equation across the top of a sheet of paper; write the name of each category, leaving plenty of room beside it; then follow these instructions.

1. **In each category, list at least five of your strengths.** Include all "bad habits" that have the potential to reap a positive reward. If you act without thinking and make a lot of mistakes, for example, you might be a great risk-taker or big-picture thinker. I often steal the center of attention from my friends. And although I am trying to be more conscious of this behavior, I also recognize that it gives me the courage to speak in front of hundreds of people. Since personal traits have different appearances and effects depending on external circumstances, do not be too quick to write off any aspect of yourself. Use the examples in figure 1–1, on page 34, as a guide.

    If you have trouble coming up with five strengths in any category, try to figure out why. Did someone once tell you that it is vain to acknowledge your strengths? As a child, did you believe that sounding conceited was wrong? Do you realize that a common definition of conceit is, "the excessive appreciation of one's worth or virtue"? Regardless of what you thought as a child, begin now to excessively appreciate your worth, to unabashedly claim your powers.

2. **Ask others for input, and add these strengths to your lists.** Other people—friends, your partner, a coworker, your boss, even casual acquaintances—may see inspiring aspects in you that you yourself have overlooked or misinterpreted. For example, one of my clients thinks that "doing nothing" means he is lazy. I see him as willing to take time to rest and reflect. Similarly, some of *your* perceived weaknesses may be strengths in disguise. Just because someone dubbed you with a negative label years ago does not mean you must continue to accept it. Albert Einstein and Mark Twain were kicked out of school and labeled "stupid." In reality, these geniuses were bored and preferred to contemplate worlds beyond the classroom.

   While gathering input from people you know, you might be pleasantly surprised by what you learn. It may shift your perspective on the spot. Any time someone gives you valuable information about yourself, accept it graciously, with a simple "thank you," before adding it to the appropriate list.

3. **For the next ten days, keep a log of your productive conversations and positive accomplishments.** Next to each entry, identify the personal qualities that contributed to its success. Add these strengths to your lists. Your daily victory log will help you end each day on a positive note, revealing strengths you might not otherwise take credit for having. Review your actions, then give yourself the compliments you deserve.

4. **Read your lists aloud each day until you have them memorized.** Committing your powers to memory will give you the confidence needed to make good decisions and glide more smoothly through your day. As author George Bernard Shaw said, "This is the true joy in life, being recognized by yourself as the mighty one."

Figure 1–1

A Sample Personal Power Inventory

KP + RP + IP = PP

Knowledge Power (KP)	Education, life experiences, attentiveness, open-mindedness, intuition, willingness to learn, willingness to forgive, willingness to not be right and to admit mistakes, risk-taking, creativity, broad perspective, observation skills, reading, listening, experiencing the present
Relationship Power (RP)	Active listening, communication skills, empathy, compassion, interest, desire to give, ability to receive, appreciation of differences, unconditional respect, responsibility, ability to show love, care for personal appearance, pleasing facial expressions, positive energy
Inner Power (IP)	Courage, conviction, commitment, calm under pressure, love of life, love of others, love of self, sense of humor, playfulness, flexibility, decisiveness, determination, commitment to truth, vulnerability, graciousness, sensitivity, generosity, loyalty, honesty, curiosity, faith, awareness, enthusiasm, appreciation, peacefulness, patience, joy

While reviewing your inventory, remember that there is no ideal combination of powers, since each listing is unique to the individual who compiled it. Remember, too, that what you lack can be developed through practice and meditation. Any time you encounter a quality you would like to add to your inventory, make it your "theme of the month." During the next four weeks, focus on "being" this new quality. Be a great sense of humor, be compassionate, or be courageous. Write the word on index cards and tape them to your calendar, your bathroom mirror, the dashboard of your car. The following month, choose another quality to add. After a month in which you have focused on a particular trait, your behavior will begin to exhibit the new mental patterns that your subconscious has been creating. You will then have the capacity to be the power you've admired in others.

As your personal power inventory grows, assess it on a regular basis—monthly, if possible. This simple review of the powers you have developed is, on its own, likely to increase your self-esteem and joy.

Taking Your Powers with You

A couple of years ago, I traded in my little sports car for a big truck. The first time I drove the truck, I was amazed at the power that surged through me. I felt bigger than everyone. No one could hurt me.

Every day I read my personal power inventory, I feel like I did during that first ride in my truck. And any time I am afraid to place a phone call, face someone at a meeting, or speak to a large group of people, I look at my inventory. I have learned that by taking my powers with me into each day, I can't go wrong.

The same is likely to hold true for you. So keep your power inventory handy—by your bed, in your desk, taped to your wallet or purse. Don't be caught powerless. Gather your forces and keep them with you every step of the way.

Knowing that my powers impelled me to climb out of the darkness of crime, drug addiction, and self-hatred, I now stand in the light of possibility ... most of the time. Recently, while addressing the subject of claiming our power before an audience of 600 people, I began to walk in and out of the spotlight. I would step out of the light to avoid the glare, then quickly return so as not to be in the dark. I had to laugh at the metaphoric enactment of how we dance in and out of our powerful selves.

Many women, especially, have an unfortunate tendency to move into the shadows. In our desire to nurture, we often step back to let others take the limelight. If this is true of you, and if you are unaccustomed to rising to your potential for your own sake, then do it for the benefit of those younger and less experienced. In author Marianne Williamson's words, "Your playing small doesn't serve the world. There is nothing enlightened about shrinking so that other people won't feel insecure around you."

The world needs more role models. Our daughters, especially, need to know strong women. Courageous women taking steps toward leadership require your support, not your envy or criticism. "And as we let our own light shine," Williamson adds, "we unconsciously give other people permission to do the same. As we are liberated from our own fear, our presence automatically liberates others." Rather than stepping out of the limelight, stand tall in the glow with outstretched arms.

As you do, remind yourself that exhibiting personal powers does not convey arrogance. Note the distinction between confidence and arrogance. Whereas *confidence* has you relying on yourself, *arrogance* compels you to compare yourself with others. Confidence can usher in fears; but when it does, the trust you have in yourself will move you forward despite them. On an even brighter note, when your confidence is solid you do not have to win or be right to feel good about yourself; you know you have done your best under the circumstances. Further, confidence leaves no room for failure. Mistakes become simply an indication that there is more to learn. And triumph is so sweet when you do win, because it's a personal victory.

Arrogance, on the other hand, propagates feelings of superiority that drain the joy from our experience. When you are in the grip of arrogance, challenges pose a threat. Failure breeds anger. Mistakes beget self-punishment. Triumph generates pious self-righteousness or outright indignation.

To capture your rapture, you will need to sit on a foundation of confidence. Identify your powers. Store them in your heart. Then act in good faith. Face uncomfortable situations with the belief that they hold a payoff for you—in terms of learning, if not success. Before long, you will be basking in the moment.

DISAPPEARING YOUR FEARS

Whereas claiming your powers adds structural support to your foundation, disappearing your fears eliminates the cracks and crevices that may at any moment give way beneath you. Fears of physical danger serve as valuable signals. Yet all other fears are apt to bump you back from focusing on "being" to obsessing over "doing."

Behind every fear unrelated to a physical threat is a lie, and lies are thieves that rob us of our power. Whenever you hear yourself say, "No, I can't (won't, don't, mustn't) do that, more likely than not a lie is filling your head with fear. Identify it as a lie and you disappear the fear.

To recognize lies before they wreak havoc, refer to figure 1–2, "The

FIGURE 1–2

The Top Ten Lies We Tell Ourselves

1. "I'm so stupid (too boring, a loser, a failure)."

2. "I don't deserve to have a life overflowing with rewards (money, love, caring friends)."

3. "I'm not good (pretty, handsome, tall, thin, strong) enough."

4. "I can't learn how to do that."
   Female version: "I can't do technical stuff."
   Male version: "I can't be sensitive."

5. "I can't make enough money doing what I love."

6. "I'm too old."

7. "No one will like me when they get to know the *real* me."

8. "I'll do it someday when I have enough time (money)."

9. "People will be afraid and jealous of me if I step into my full power."

10. "Days filled with passion and joy is a pipe dream—life is about sacrifice, caring for others, and minor pleasures resulting from hard work."

Top Ten Lies We Tell Ourselves," as often as you wish. These are the lies that most often cause fissures in our foundation.

Lie number one, "I'm so stupid (too boring, a loser, a failure)," implies a perception of the world as two dimensional—good-bad, pretty-ugly, rich-poor—and of ourselves as inferior. It's shorthand for "I fail to consider the fact that I'm multifaceted, with at least as many strengths as weaknesses. I focus only on areas I see as deficient for the occasion." Focusing on our soft spots leads to a fear of risk-taking, which causes us to miss opportunities for growth.

For eleven years I worked at high-tech companies despite a lack of technical training. In fact, as often as I could I avoided taking math and science classes in school. If, when offered my first high-tech training job, I focused on how stupid I felt in the presence of technical minds, I would never have accepted the position. Instead, I focused on my skills in instructional design, interpersonal relationships, and listening. Relying on these competencies, I created effective training programs, filling in the missing pieces of information by drawing on the expertise of the technical wizards in my midst. I was *not* too stupid to work in a high-tech company. In fact, I was generously rewarded for using the knowledge I had.

Calling ourselves stupid is a good excuse to avoid taking risks. This is true not only at work but also in relationships. If you instead admit that someone might find you interesting, you eliminate the excuse and move beyond past experiences that kept you from taking a chance.

Dissolve a lie of inadequacy and you can toss aside the crutch you've been leaning on. Getting rid of the crutch lets you experience long dormant or undiscovered parts of yourself. Knowing that you are not too stupid to tackle a prospective task, your feeble "I know so little" becomes "I have a bit of wisdom in some areas, I'm pretty confident in others, and I can always learn more." In other words, you begin to concentrate on your strengths instead of your weaknesses.

Lie number two, "I don't deserve to have a life overflowing with rewards (money, love, caring friends)," goes even deeper. It assumes that we are not good enough to have a full life because we are defective human beings who have done bad things. This lie breeds a fear of success, seen regularly among people who sabotage their careers and relationships just as circumstances become harmonious and productive. Looking for things to break down, they eventually experience a collapse.

To invalidate this lie, ask yourself if you know anyone who is *not* defective and has *never* done something bad. Then begin to see yourself as a fortunate, growing being with unlimited chances for improvement.

Perfection is an illusion—an unreal target we can never achieve despite our most valiant efforts. Who you are right now, with all your flaws, is a perfect seed for beginning to be someone new. By regarding each day as a fresh start, you can forgive yourself for past misdeeds, ask others to forgive you, then focus on the opportunities spread out before you. Feeling undeserving denies the talents you've been given. Say thank you for your life by grabbing your gifts and running with them.

Lie number three, "I'm not good (pretty, handsome, tall, thin, strong) enough," fosters equally immobilizing fears. We have Hollywood and advertising to thank for the outrageous standards we use to evaluate our own beauty. Although society gives top scores to outer appearance, inner radiance is much more powerful. Show the world you care about yourself by taking the time to look your best, then strive to be beautiful from the inside out. Radiant energy is attractive even in the morning when we roll out of bed. Remember that any limitations you declare are in fact yours. Refuse to label your physical characteristics as limitations and the lie is history.

Lie number four, "I can't learn how to do that," spawns a fear of failure. Had I succumbed to the belief that I was technically incompetent, I would never have even considered a job with a computer company, for I would have been too fearful of floundering. As it turned out, within two years of signing on I was immersed in technical terminology and had become the international product training manager. I traveled extensively, teaching salesmen the benefits of our products. By eradicating the lie of incompetence, you too can augment your future and realize your dreams.

If you subscribe to the lie that you're insensitive, you are probably fearful of revealing your emotions and block out those expressed by others. People who claim insensitivity have many rationalizations for their resistance to feelings, often blaming the lack of time or poor role modeling. Sensitivity asks us only to quiet our minds and listen carefully to what other people say, all the while observing their nonverbal behavior. Try paying closer attention to others, and see how many unspoken thoughts and feelings you pick up on. Could it be that you are actually highly sensitive? When we stop claiming responsibility for other people's emotions and quit worrying about what they will think if they glimpse at ours, we clear the way to more meaningful relationships. Learn to view sensitivity as a mainstay of good communication. Be proud of the intuition you develop through listening.

Lie number four also generates the foremost human fear—speaking in public. If you are convinced you cannot speak in front of a group, you are probably telling yourself that as a public speaker you will look and sound like a complete idiot. In other words, this lie has you thinking that to succeed you have to be the most interesting and eloquent speaker in town. The truth is, most people see only a fraction of the fear we're feeling. And if we stumble over our words, they are more apt to sympathize with us than condemn us.

To rid yourself of the lie, tell yourself that what you have to say is important. Then stand up and practice. Take a class in public speaking. Head to your nearest Toastmasters Club. Volunteer to speak whenever you can. Soon, your worries about failing will be a fading memory.

Lie number five, "I can't make enough money doing what I love," provokes a fear of not being good at what we're passionate about. We think: "If I write books, no one will read them" or "If I paint pictures, they won't find a buyer even at a garage sale." Yet stories abound about people turning their passions into profit. Heidi, a friend who left her corporate job, built a business on her love for cooking; Heidi's Home Catering is now a huge success. Jenny, who started a jewelry business in her family room, now sells her handiwork in boutiques worldwide. Rahla loves to make people laugh, so she organizes "playshops" for major corporations, demonstrating how humor can improve productivity in the workplace. Gary turned his love for gardening and spiritual mythology into a landscape design venture specializing in sacred spaces.

Although displaying our passion leaves us vulnerable to critique, suppressing it erodes our happiness. Extinguish the lie by believing you can make enough money doing what you are passionate about. The critique will lose its importance. Then, starting out small, begin to do what you love. Show your work around. Talk about it as often as you can. You will find people appreciating and supporting your efforts.

Lie number six, "I'm too old," becomes less justified as longevity increases. Why? Because the term "too old" has little bearing in today's world. Although as time passes we may develop physical limitations and reduced mental acuity, nothing stops us from earning doctorates in our sixties, writing best-sellers in our seventies, and marrying a true love in our eighties. Stamp out the lie and you disappear the fear of self-fulfillment.

Lie number seven, "No one will like me when they get to know the *real* me," lurks beneath fears of intimacy and rejection. If you adhere to this belief about yourself, you most likely work hard at avoiding whatever might bring you shame and humiliation. Rather than experience these feelings, you may go into hiding—refusing to share genuine warmth in your relationships, turning away prestigious jobs, and feeling lonely as a result. In protecting yourself from harm, you've sequestered your heart and limited your ability to feel powerfully alive. To reverse the situation, ask a close friend to remind you that the unique you is much more lovable than the shallow facade you've been presenting. Abolish the lie and you discover that the most negative judgments about you come from your own head rather than from other people.

Elayne Savage, author of *Don't Take It Personally*, recommends overcoming the fear of rejection through self-soothing behaviors. When you make a mistake, laugh at yourself before anyone else can. Do so in a kind, painless way. When you are nervous, calm yourself by stroking your hand, arm, or stomach. Review your lists of personal powers. Ask a friend to remind you of them from time to time. As you feel stronger, you'll be more inclined to share the real you with others.

Lie number eight, "I'll do it someday when I have enough time (money)," is doubly damaging, since the words *someday* and *enough* spark two fears: that what we have now is insufficient and that it will never be adequate to warrant taking a risk. Symphonies go uncomposed and exotic destinations unvisited, shingles are never hung and friendships never made—all because of an outlook steeped in scarcity. To eradicate the lie, first remind yourself that "someday" is not a day of the week and offers nothing tangible to aim for. Give yourself a target year or month for bringing your desire to fruition. Then break it into manageable pieces and commit to starting with what you already have. No matter what you wish for, you can always *begin* to manifest it today.

Second, define "enough." Most often, the amount of time or money a task demands is not as daunting as we may think. Talk to others who have written symphonies, traveled to faraway places, launched successful home businesses, or developed an extensive network of friends. They will tell you how much time and money you need, and will provide tips on how to get the most for less.

Lie number nine, "People will be afraid and jealous of me if I step into my full power," propagates fears of self-expression and of exploring personal potential. The truth is, the world needs strong people to emulate. Diminishing your light only deprives others of it. Self-sacrifice is not noble; forfeiting your desires in order to please others drains the joy from your life and impedes the development of theirs. Through self-actualization, however, you become a model for others. Stepping into your power invites them to step into theirs.

If you believe lie number ten, "Days filled with passion and joy is a pipe dream—life is about sacrifice, caring for others, and minor pleasures resulting from hard work," you may fear happiness. You may also think that happiness is disruptive, or harmful. To disappear the fear, get rid of the lie by ingesting these chapters with an open mind. Practice the exercises. Work with the techniques that amplify your happiness. Accept all proof that the expression of happiness can enrich your life. Then spread your wings and see where you go.

Many more lies also exist, fueling a variety of other fears. As you identify those you hold dear and realize how untrue they really are, you disarm the impact they have on your brain. Simultaneously this awareness will vanish your fears, liberating you to choose who you *want* to be. If you would like help in disappearing your fears, contact a personal coach, therapist, counselor, or spiritual advisor. To find a certified coach, see the referral services listed on page 236.

ACKNOWLEDGING YOUR NEEDS

Needs are a part of being human. Many people have, at the very least, a need for control, for appreciation and respect, for financial security, and for freedom. Although there is nothing wrong with having these needs, the voice of an *unacknowledged* need can be strong enough to damage our confidence. If you are afraid to act because you think the results will be less than satisfying, or if you defend yourself so fiercely that you alienate others, you are most likely being plagued by hidden needs. Unrecognized needs distort our perception, affect our decision-making abilities, drown out our desires, and cause opportunities to pass us by.

To stop unacknowledged needs from exhausting your powers, the first step is to face them squarely. Some, such as the need for harmony, you may decide to feed until they are satisfied. Others, such as the need to win, you may want to "downgrade" by reducing to a nice-to-have-but-I-won't-let-it-bother-me-anymore status. Or you may want to release them entirely. With this task accomplished, you will be free to embrace the pleasure of being.

Confronting your needs may take practice, especially if you have learned to deny their existence. To begin to uncover them, try the following three methods.

Immediate Identification
Running head-on into an unruly need can leave you feeling frustrated, angry, disappointed, or ashamed. However, if you refrain from pursuing a dream for fear of encountering an unaddressed need, you will also feel frustrated, angry, disappointed, or ashamed. To resolve this dilemma, identify your needs now, before they become more unmanageable. The exercise shown in figure 1–3 can help you prevent a surprise collision.

Figure 1–3

Unacknowledged Needs That Erode Confidence

Following is a list of twelve of the most damaging unacknowledged needs.* Circle those that are important to you, then do what you can to satisfy, downgrade, or release them.

I need:	Acceptance	Harmony
	Acknowledgment	To be in control
	Respect	To feel important
	Prosperity	To feel accomplished
	Appreciation	To win
	Consistency	To be loved

*Adapted from Coach University's Needless Assessment

Root Cause Analysis

Root cause analysis, a method borrowed from manufacturing plants, can help you determine the needs that are driving your most problematic behaviors. When a difficulty arises in manufacturing settings, process engineers analyze data to find the root cause. When they fix what they see on the surface only, the error tends to recur. Yet when they look below the surface for the real cause of the problem, they can effect enduring changes. Likewise, if you try to correct a confidence problem by quitting your job or relationship, you may at first feel good, then something is apt to send you reeling down the same hole of self-doubt. Going to the cause of your unwanted behavior, as described in figure 1–4, will help you fill the hole.

FIGURE 1–4

Performing a Root Cause Analysis

Do this exercise as soon as possible after acting in a way that causes you emotional discomfort. If you cannot do it at the time of your reaction, find a quiet place shortly afterward to conduct your investigation. Answer the questions as truthfully as possible.

- What or how were you feeling at the time of your unwanted behavior? Circle the correct responses.

Vengeful	Irate	Worthless
Hurt	Frustrated	Annoyed
Stuck	Misunderstood	Lonely
Disappointed	Irritated	Frantic

- What personal needs may have been ignored? Review the list of unacknowledged needs in figure 1–3 to see which ones precipitated your response. Answering this question will take you below surface events to the real cause of your feelings and reactions.

- Next time these needs appear, how might you respond?

Once you begin to identify the needs that most often cause you to react with anger or pain, you will be able to name them the moment they appear, allowing you to choose how you *want* to respond instead of reacting blindly. For instance, rather than pouting or getting mad when your partner ignores your good work, you could say, "Oh, there's my need for acknowledgment again. I can ask for the feedback I want."

For each need that is important to you, decide how best to manage it. If possible, find ways to meet the need. You can ask others to help you satisfy the need or you can fulfill it yourself by setting goals and claiming your powers. Your other options are to downgrade it or release it.

If, for example, you find you have a need *to be in control* but your position at work is restrictive, you can master the need in one of several ways. To satisfy it, you might decide to run for office in a professional association you belong to, or to coach the company's softball team. Or you might ask your manager to help you set goals so that in the future you will be able to meet your need to be in control. If you determine that the need does not serve you right now—if you are making enough money to support your family, prefer not to add more activities to an already busy schedule, and have the opportunity to move to another company next year—it might be best to downgrade the need, knowing that it will be met in due course.

After downgrading a need, be patient since frustration may occasionally rear its head. If you cannot find the time to write your novel, consider this the year to build your business instead, or to focus more strongly on nurturing your children. Trust that next year there may be time to create your masterpiece. As novelist Anna Quindlen says, "You probably can have it all. Just not all at the same time."

Releasing a need, on the other hand, calls for focus and perseverance. Athletes, for instance, perform better once they've released the need to win. To let it go, they learn to focus on the present moment, on the joy of their performance, instead of on how they are stacking up against the competition. A good way to release a need is by mentally surrounding it with a blue bubble and letting it float away. Then choose to be peaceful, creative, or successful instead of needy.

A History Lesson

A third method to use in identifying your needs invites you to examine your past behavior. Unearthing a historical need, as is described in figure 1–5, can help you recognize a current one. It can also help you discharge stagnant emotions related to the old unacknowledged need—feelings that are distorting your perception of present circumstances.

While exploring my past behavior, I have uncovered a number of needs. For example, I found that I need my work to be appreciated. When I give written material to an editor, before anything else I like positive feedback, which increases my receptivity to suggestions for improvement. I also need respect, so I ask people to hear me out and acknowledge my ideas before presenting me with theirs. And I have a need to be in control, although I have at times learned to let this one go.

FIGURE 1–5

Completing a History Lesson

Understanding your history allows you to leave it in the past, seeing people and situations of the present in a new light. To dig up long-buried and still hungry needs, follow these steps. Repeat them for every memory that still feels painful or unresolved.

- Recall a time when you felt one of the emotions circled in figure 1–4. Recount the incident out loud, either to yourself or to a good friend who is able to quietly listen to you. Be sure to express how irate, frustrated, or lonely you felt.

- Looking over your list of unacknowledged needs in figure 1–3, see if you can identify the culprit. (It may be an unlisted need.) If you cannot determine the root cause for the emotion, continue to retell the story until the need emerges.

- To prevent the offending need from showing up in the present, find a way to satisfy, downgrade, or release it.

Knowing what my needs are, I can better choose my responses and clear energy-draining forces from my life. It is in the clearing that joy emerges.

Using Humor to Deflate Needs

In addition to satisfying, downgrading, or releasing our needs, there are times we can deflate them through the use of humor. The less "air" we give them, the less devastating they are.

Imagine that you have a need to be appreciated or accepted, and you are to be the keynote speaker at an important conference. You have determined that the last thing you want to do is trip over the microphone cord on your way to the stage, for it would cause the audience to discount your message. Instead of getting flustered by your need, you might decide in advance to laugh at yourself and *thank* the audience for allowing you to "trip over your words." A friend told me about a lawyer who used this strategy after realizing halfway through his plea to the jury that his fly was open: he zipped it up and announced, "Obviously, I have nothing to hide in this case." Maintaining a lightness of being will keep you intact—safe from the damaging effects of your needs.

Lightness permeates once you realize that if your needs are not met, your world will not cave in. After all, if you fail to get what you want—the promotion you desire, the date, your opinion taken seriously, praise from your manager, or applause from your team—will it really matter? Most likely, the only injury you will suffer is a bruised ego. And if you are aware of your powers and prepared to laugh at the blunders, you are sure to heal quickly.

Helen Alfredsson, a championship golfer, pokes fun at herself whenever she is attacked by her needs to win and to be acknowledged. Once, she was playing golf with actor Sidney Poitier, who appeared considerably reserved. Aware that men prefer to play golf with men, Helen felt her needs for winning and acknowledgment begin to wage war in her head, weakening her game. Add the intimidation of playing with such a famous person, and her confidence quickly spiraled downhill. The second hole was a nightmare. Before playing the third hole, she removed the windshield on her cart to get some sun, laying the sheet of plastic at her feet. As she walked across the fairway, however, the cart took off on its own. Helen ran in fast pursuit. The cart crashed into a bush, at which point she realized that the windshield had fallen on the gas pedal. She began to laugh so hysterically that her return to the hole seemed to take an eternity. Fortunately, it no longer mattered what Mr. Poitier thought of her, for the worst had already happened. And she had survived. She went on to shoot a respectable round, giving Sidney Poitier a story he would never forget.

Lighten up. Laugh at your overprotective brain. Take the air out of your needs so that your confidence can rise. Life can be much more fun.

TAKING CARE OF YOURSELF

Your personal powers require a vessel that is impeccably well cared for. This is a task only you can do. How? By assessing your current level of self-care, heightening it, and making the shifts in perspective needed to keep it in top condition.

Homing In on Self-Care

Passion, joy, and confidence rapidly lose their luster to noise pollution, sleep deprivation, poor nutrition, excessive conflict, lack of money, and a shortage of friends. To see what condition your vessel is in, complete the checklist in figure 1–6. Then tally up the boxes you've checked. Set goals to accomplish the remaining tasks, one at a time, until your score reaches at least 35. As your score increases, notice how much more energy you have. Clear out the corrosion. The flame that warms you will burn much brighter.

This checklist will help you concentrate on your environmental, physical, mental, financial, and relationship well-being. Chapter 2 offers techniques for coping with the emotional wreckage left by disappointment, hardship, and loss. Suggestions for improving your radiance and energy follow.

You Come First

In an airplane emergency, who gets the oxygen first—the adult or the child? We are instructed to strap on our mask and *then* care for our child. We cannot help another if we're gasping for air. Life is similar: while suffering, suffocating, starved, sapped, or scared, we are in no condition to assist a friend in need, much less able to take pleasure in the moment. Simply put, healthy "selfishness" is necessary for bringing joy to others as well as to ourselves.

FIGURE 1–6

Self-Care Checklist

Read each question below. If your answer is "yes," place a check in the box beside it.

Environment

❏ Are your home and office clean? Are they clutter-free?

❏ Are your appliances in working order?

❏ Does your home offer a peaceful, quiet place where you can relax and think?

❏ Are backup systems in place in the event of an electric failure, computer crash, or car breakdown?

❏ Is your home equipped with a smoke detector, fire extinguisher, and speed dial for emergency calls?

❏ Do you store enough home-care and office supplies to keep errands to a minimum?

❏ Do you find the colors and wall decor in your home and office pleasing? Is the temperature comfortable?

Physical Health

❏ Do you get enough sleep each night? Are you ever too tired to function well?

❏ Is your bed comfortable? Does your office chair provide adequate back support?

❏ Is your diet nutritionally sound? Do you eat enough fresh, healthful food?

❏ Do you exercise at least three times a week?

❏ Is your cholesterol count within the normal range?

❏ Do you drink at least eight glasses of filtered water each day?

❏ Are you drug-free and caffeine-free?

❏ Do you keep your sugar intake to a minimum?

Mental Health

❏ Do you wake up looking forward to your day?

❏ Do you fall asleep at night with gratitude in your heart?

❏ Do you take at least three refreshing and energizing vacations each year?

❏ Is there someone in your life who hugs you regularly?

❏ Do you arrive at least five minutes early for appointments?

❏ Do you drive at a gentle pace?

❏ Do you promise only what you can deliver?

❏ Do you regularly explore new ways of perceiving and being in the world?

Money

❏ Are your debts paid off?

❏ Do you save at least 10 percent of your income?

❏ Are you compensated adequately for your work?

❏ Do you have a reserve of funds to cover home, car, or health emergencies?

❏ Are you amply insured for your home, car, and health?

❏ Do you invest in personal development to increase your earnings?

❏ Do you have a special knowledge or skill that gives you job security?

❏ Do you have a reputable and knowledgeable financial advisor?

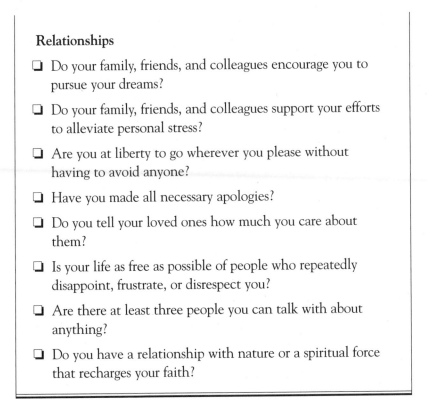

Relationships

❏ Do your family, friends, and colleagues encourage you to pursue your dreams?

❏ Do your family, friends, and colleagues support your efforts to alleviate personal stress?

❏ Are you at liberty to go wherever you please without having to avoid anyone?

❏ Have you made all necessary apologies?

❏ Do you tell your loved ones how much you care about them?

❏ Is your life as free as possible of people who repeatedly disappoint, frustrate, or disrespect you?

❏ Are there at least three people you can talk with about anything?

❏ Do you have a relationship with nature or a spiritual force that recharges your faith?

Remember always to prize yourself as your greatest asset. Honor the body that carries your soul. Nourish the mind that directs your actions. Delight your senses. Soothe your emotions. Relieve your conscience. Sleep and eat well. Drink more water. Let others clean up after you once in a while. Jump-start your body with exercise, then pamper it with a massage, a bath, and plenty of sleep. Energy spent caring for yourself is energy gained. Only while practicing rigorous self-care can you live "the good life."

After crossing the worst of the Nefud desert, Lawrence of Arabia discovered that one of the men with him at the start, Gasem, had not made it. As Lawrence turned back to retrieve the man, tribal leader Sherif Ali ordered him to stay, explaining, "His time has come, Lawrence. It is written."

Lawrence ignored Ali. Confident that he could endure the desert's brutality, Lawrence descended into the hell of sand and heat. He found Gasem. They both returned alive.

Ali, looking in awe at Lawrence, said, "Truly for some men, nothing is written until they write it."

You are writing your book of life. "Be" your powers, vanish your fears, tame your needs, and take impeccable care of yourself. Completing this work is like strengthening your legs. Hardy muscles make for an easier and more enjoyable excursion.

CHAPTER 2

Weathering the Storms

When Goliath came against the Israelites,
the soldiers all thought, "He's so big
we can never kill him."
David looked at the same giant and thought,
"He's so big, how can I miss?"

—Russ Johnson

"I'll huff and I'll puff and I'll blow your house down." Do you ever feel like the three little pigs—utterly vulnerable as you anticipate the wrath of the big, bad wolf? Crisis can rock our lives like a tornado. Hurricanes hit, gales pound, and floods course through our best laid plans. How well do we weather the storms? Although a strong foundation can minimize the damage, the true test comes in how quickly we are able to rebuild our capacity for joy.

RESILIENCE

Most people who face catastrophe either shut down—physically, emotionally, or spiritually—or summon the power to heal. But what gives one woman the strength to beat cancer and go on to become a champion body-builder while her alcoholic sister cannot manage to hold a job? Although psychological studies that explain reactive tendencies disagree on many points, the data consistently shows that people who bounce back from adversity are primarily those who believe they can. And, as indicated by the 1998 National Study of Daily Experiences conducted at the University of Arizona, they believe they can because they have learned how to cope with everyday upsets.

In fact, the greatest predictor of effective crisis management is how quickly we return to joy when faced with traffic jams, ringing telephones, screaming toddlers, aging parents, computer viruses, human viruses, broken bones, and broken promises. Similarly, the sum of these daily glitches and stressors is what tests our foundations the most. Small storms can wear us thin, causing more damage over time than bigger ones. Why? Because the resulting impatience, anger, and resentment have a way of slowly and permanently eroding us. People who quickly repair the cracks, leaks, and rifts can sleep comfortably through winter storms.

According to the 1998 National Study of Daily Experiences, the incidents that most commonly cause stress and suffering have nothing to do with disaster. Instead, participants claimed the culprits were burnt dinners, hunting for parking spaces, running late, haggling with rude neighbors, and disagreeing with people they expected to enrich their lives, such as friends, relatives, children, coworkers, and spouses. "It doesn't matter if you're a graduate student trying to juggle studies with a social life, a parent shuttling kids between school and soccer games, or an executive dealing with an unruly staff," says David Almeida, assistant professor of family studies and coconductor of the ten-year study. "Daily stresses affect physical and psychological health as much as big events such as a divorce or death of a spouse." Their cumulative effect is constant headaches, backaches, anxiety, depression, and fatigue—conditions that leave little room for pleasure.

Almeida's most surprising discovery came at the end of a round of studies. After eight consecutive days of talking with participants about their routines, he found that most expressed remorse that the interviews were about to end. "They didn't have anyone to call them up every night to talk about job promotions, changing relationships, computers crashing, or partners who wanted too much or too little sex." This unexpected response alerted Almeida to the profound isolation that people feel in today's culture, even when they work and live with others. Loneliness, boredom, conflicts, and interruptions override the impact of relaxation, a simplified household life, working out with punching bags, and other popularized stress-reduction techniques. Relief requires at least one friend we can talk, laugh, and cry with on a regular basis. In short, weathering the storms requires heart-to-heart human contact.

Determined to uncover the secrets of enjoying life, Leonard Poon, PhD, formed a research team in 1993 to study active, healthy centenarians. The team found that the most common characteristic shared by the independent 100 year olds was an optimistic attitude. "It's a case of mind over body," Dr. Poon says. "Even when their bodies have deteriorated, their minds will them to go forward."

The centenarians in this study displayed three primary traits: an ability to adapt to loss; a passionate commitment to a job, organization, or person; and an active lifestyle involving other people, even when confined to a wheelchair. In other words, vibrant centenarians have a sense of purpose and choose to go on living instead of focusing on negativity as they approach death. Trait number one, the ability to adapt to loss, implies a well-cultivated urge toward resilience—a finely honed ability to accept, adapt to, and bounce back from hard times, returning as quickly as possible to the pleasure of each moment.

According to Gary Zukav, author of *The Seat of the Soul*, "You can just as easily laugh and play while you grow as become serious and overwhelmed." Having a mid-laugh crisis rather than a midlife crisis is a sure sign of resilience. Four impulses that nourish this trait are desire, willingness, creativity, and courage, all of which are needed for climbing out of a rut.

DESIRE

Before we see positive changes in our lives, we have to *want* them to occur. As elementary as this principle may sound, however, it is rarely practiced. We are instead afraid of change—a fear that keeps us rooted in unhealthy situations and behavioral patterns.

But wanting changes to occur, even talking about them, is only a start. We must also prepare to *take action* toward manifesting them.

Many bright and perceptive people have planted themselves in suffocating jobs that they feel incapable of leaving, much as they would like to. For some, anger or loss eventually catapults them into action; for others, the anger festers, causing them, as Walt Whitman said, to die with their music in them. It is better to be ignorant of possibilities than to be haunted by their existence.

Desire has us ready to admit that we are capable of moving to another level. For example, on the day I resigned from my last corporate position, scores of people came to say goodbye. None asked me to stay, much to my ego's chagrin; instead, they praised me for being courageous. Six months later, when a former coworker spotted me at the grocery store, she hugged me on sight. "Thank you," she said, "you showed me that the handcuffs weren't locked." My leaving, she explained, had forced her to recognize that she, too, could leave. She hated her job. She felt humiliated and tired there. Yet for years it had been easier to acquiesce to her circumstances than take responsibility for her happiness. When I left, she geared up for action. Realizing that if I could do it she could too, she dusted off her wings and flew.

Children see the world around them as responsible for their upsets. Troubled teenagers blame their parents, teachers, and others for the injustices they experience. Most of us adults, although intellectually aware that we are responsible for our own lives, tend to subscribe to this belief only when things are going well. We prefer to attribute our unhappiness to the company, Mom or Dad, the children, or our lover. We wallow in gloom as if we have earned the right to be miserable.

Blaming and complaining injure the soul. Free-reining negativity eventually spawns rabid infections of self-pity. The poison travels, affecting our vision and our mobility. Soon, all that is left to do from our envenomed perspective is sit back and accept our deplorable job, relationship, or other sorry predicament. The answer is not always to leave; yet that may be our only perceived option, since we rarely see growth-promoting alternatives while feeling angry or depressed. "The ingenuity of self-deception is inexhaustible," wrote essayist Hannah Moore in 1881.

Ultimately, the lie that gives rise to the fear of change is that someone else controls our lives. To disarm the fear, we need to accept that we have chosen our difficult situations. In accepting ourselves as agents, we remove the veil of self-deception and give voice to our hearts' desires. If we wait for the boss to change his mind, the city to redirect the traffic flow, our partner to chill out, or our friends to stop complaining, we will forever be victims. If instead we allow desire to prepare us for action, we become creators. Even choosing to do nothing for a period of time carries more weight than turning our power over to others.

In short, to be resilient we must *desire* to improve our situation. Rather than view a personal hardship as someone else's responsibility, we claim accountability for it, commit ourselves to positive growth, and exercise the power we have to shape our reality. With desire, we ride from misery to joy.

Do you want more passion in your life? Are you ready to make changes in both your physical and mental worlds to achieve it? If so, acknowledge that you can ameliorate your circumstances. Decide that when opportunities appear you will open your mouth and speak up, move your feet, and reach for what you want. Light a fire inside so that you won't freeze up. Then announce your desires daily to keep that flame alive.

WILLINGNESS

An old riddle asks, "If three frogs are sitting on a lily pad and one decides to jump, how many frogs are left behind?" The answer is "three," because deciding to jump is not the same as jumping. Here is another riddle: "If three people are sitting on a couch crying about their miserable lives and one declares his desire to change his circumstances, how many people are left sitting on the couch?" Once again, the answer is "three." If the first ingredient of resilience is desire, the second is a *willingness to act* on our desires.

Once we have publicized an intention, even if only to ourselves, we can no longer remain unconscious of the pain or drabness of our situation. In fact, the truth becomes more apparent every day, and if we do not choose to change our circumstances we are apt to become helpless witnesses of our own disasters. Therefore, once you decide that a change is necessary, take action quickly—before losing that job, getting sick, receiving the divorce papers, or wrecking the car. As

Mark Twain said, "Even if you're on the right track, if you don't move you'll get run over."

What if storms have already hit and your life is currently plagued with worries and frustration? Doris Helge, PhD, author of *Transforming Pain into Power*, writes, "Years ago, I was fortunate enough to be involved in a painful divorce, was experiencing a health problem, was bored with my job, and had no real friendships. Later, I was blessed with an unexpected certified letter in which I was given thirty days in which to vacate a rental home at a time when an automobile accident left me unable to walk for a number of months." The key words in Dr. Helge's account are *fortunate* and *blessed*, suggesting that she views her misfortune as a gift. "The experiences compelled me to take a good look in the mirror, and work with the areas of myself that I detested," she adds. At that point she declared a willingness to forge her way through the turbulent bleakness to the light. "[The gold] shimmers expectantly during the darkest of nights," she tells us, "ready to be mined in all our painful experiences."

If pain is a signal to redirect our lives, then crisis is a fire alarm. As soon as the smoke detector goes off, it is time to announce your willingness to change. If you desire a better job, interview a variety of people in your chosen niche to find out what it takes to get there, then create a plan to become properly qualified—preferably in the near future. If you desire appreciation from your manager and peers, ask for acknowledgment before getting angry and combative. If you see no way out of your sorrow, seek help before retreating. You may feel guilty about seeking a change, especially when dealing with a family member who is sick or troubled. If so, do not let your mind stop you from reaching out for support, making a new friend, or pampering yourself with a much-needed vacation. Simultaneously, bolster your personal foundation and remind yourself that needs are not bad. Accept your needs, then find a way to add light to your life.

Willingness to set forth into the unknown is like choosing to walk through a haunted house on Halloween. We know we will face fear, confusion, and darkness. We also know there is an exit at the far end. We get scared *and* we keep walking.

Of course, some of our desires we may never fulfill. Everyone has a heart that breaks. We all have dreams just out of reach. Yet acting on each aspiration, regardless of the outcome, is far more satisfying than letting it pass us by.

What blocks willingness? Most obstructions we blame on the lack of time or money. In reality, inaction more frequently comes from a refusal to deal with our fears. Iyanla Vanzant, in her book *One Day My Soul Just Opened Up*, writes, "I was not willing to make people angry or hurt their feelings. . . . I was not willing to sound weird or stupid or like a know-it-all. I was not willing to run the risk of being wrong. I was not willing or prepared to defend myself if I were challenged. . . . I knew what needed to be done, but I was not willing to do it."

Such fears hold us captive, yet once we grapple with them they dissolve. Fear of disapproval can be vanquished as soon as we understand that other people will not always be happy with what we do or say. Indeed, some will *never* like what we do or say. Fear of making a mistake is surmountable upon the realization that we are all less than perfect. The energy spent worrying about how to please others is energy wasted.

When it comes to making decisions for ourselves, we often view our options through the prism of our parents', spouse's, or friends' opinions. Once we remove the filters formed by others' expectations of us, we can see the life that awaits us. At that point, we would do well to befriend someone who will support our willingness to stand courageously behind our desires. The greater the changes we plan to make, the more vital the role of at least one person to listen to us and cheer us on . . . and the more urgent the need for action. Every hour that we put off living for ourselves weakens our will to move.

Freeing yourself from the emotional power others have over you is like learning to walk without a crutch you have leaned on for years. "At first you will feel uncomfortable," says Jerry Minchinton, author of *Maximum Self-Esteem*, "but the longer you are without [the crutch], the stronger you will grow." After liberating yourself from the fear of what other people think, you are bound to discover a huge reservoir of energy.

Yes, you have loved ones to care for. You would rather not offend your boss. You like to make people smile. In truth, you can fulfill these objectives while pleasing *yourself*. Don't let responsibilities become excuses for ignoring your desires. "When we are finally willing to relinquish the need to live through others and acknowledge that we deserve a life of our own choosing," writes Sarah Ban Breathnach in *Something More*, "we are ready to move on and be born again . . ."

In essence, willingness is the ability to act on your desires without knowing the outcome. It is giving love without knowing if you will be loved in return. It's performing without knowing if the presentation will elicit applause. It's speaking without knowing if anyone cares to listen. To be willing is to act because it *feels right to you*. There are no pros or cons, only personal growth. Thomas Leonard, founder of Coach University, says, "What I've seen time and time again is that people who adopt this approach find new sources of energy and money, and eventually get 100 percent of their satisfaction solely from doing what they do rather than from a payoff of some sort. The payoff is great, but it's no longer the motivating factor."

The more willing you are to increase your happiness, the more adept you will be at self-care. Others may love you, support you, and urge you on. Or they may chide you and talk behind your back. In either case, hug them as you go by, marching in pursuit of your dreams.

CREATIVITY

Resilience hinges strongly on creativity—the art of using our imagination. Without it, we are doomed to stagnation. Desire is burning a hole in our soul. Willingness has us ready to dash . . . but where to? Everything looks the same as it did yesterday. Each night ends like the one before. It appears that running will only return us to where we started, just sweatier and out of breath.

When we cannot see our way out of a troubling predicament—a relationship, a job, a confirmed decision—desire and willingness can become toxic. Wanting and preparing for change amid a perceived "no exit" situation can be so antagonizing that we dive into a depression that leaves us crying, sleeping, and withering away. Yet with creativity, we begin to see beyond present circumstances and open a door to the future.

Some people attend my workshops unable to open that door. While everyone else is writing grand visions of their future, they stare blankly out the window. When I ask if they need help, they whisper that they see nothing to change in their lives. "Nothing?" I ask. "Isn't there one thing you'd like to have for yourself—one area of your life that could use some brightening up? Would you like to revive an activity or hobby you once loved, or perhaps bring back a dream you've let go of?" The strength of their "no" tells me to back off. During the afternoon break, however, they tend to tell me more. One woman burst into tears as she confided, "There's nothing I can change." We talked until we found one small step she could take. Others, a bit more optimistic, will admit at the outset, "Well, maybe there's one, but only one, thing I would change." Mentally, we join hands. I honor their courage to look outside the box.

The Critical Role of Outlook

"Your outlook determines your outcome," coach Keith Rosen told me after I had complained about a string of dates I'd been on, none very satisfying. I took his words to mean that my attitude had foreshadowed my circumstances.

"How profound," I grumbled. Conjuring up positive thoughts obviously was not going to dissolve my funk.

He explained that outlook had nothing to do with attitude, but instead meant *how far you can look out.* "When you feel as though you're stumbling through a dark tunnel," he said, "your outlook is narrow. You can't even see the end of the tunnel. But once you've crawled out and widened your angle of view, you can see the many options spread out before you, which cannot help but improve your outcome."

Keith then helped me understand the distinction between attitude and outlook. Attitude is frame of mind. Outlook is our view of the frame from where we stand, and how many pieces we can see within it. Expanding the frame does improve our attitude, but only because it increases our visibility. With an expanded outlook, "I see nothing to change" becomes "Look at all the choices I have before me." To improve my prospects, Keith suggested that if a date is not fun, the following morning I ought to wake up eager to meet a better match for myself and prepared to find this man anywhere.

Using his advice, the question I now ask in the midst of any difficult situation is, "From where I stand, are circumstances truly black or can I find a spark of possibility?" I then expand my outlook and view the situation from different perspectives. Even a shred of evidence indicating the presence of light at the end of the "tunnel" is enough to keep me moving. The more expansive my outlook is, the more choices there are within my range of vision—and the more *creative* I can be in affecting my outcome. To continually catalyze my creativity, I have become an "optionist."

It takes courage to pry open a closed mind. Yet continuing to say "no" to life soon stops it dead in its tracks. Rationalizing and defending a joyless existence keeps us nestled in a safe, mediocre, and suffocating world. Saying, "Yes, there are possibilities!" is the greatest gift you can offer yourself.

Improvisational actors are taught to say "yes" in order to keep a scene moving. Whatever it takes—deep relaxation or sheer will—they are expected to go with the flow and engage in the motion around them. So it is in life, the ultimate improvisational stage. As Twyman Towery, author of *The Wisdom of Wolves*, observes, "Things turn out for the best for the people who make the best of the way things turn out." The trick is to step into the moment with both heart and mind open to insight.

Stepping into the Present

Stepping into the present, a second catalyst for creativity, is a trick because it takes careful maneuvering and a dash of luck. Once accomplished, it manages to clear any mental state fogged by resistance. It is the solvent that lifts the glue from our feet, cleans the vapor from our eyes, and propels us toward inventiveness.

Maneuvering your way into the "now" after a setback calls for proficiency in two skills: reframing the past and redefining the present. To master them, work with the following series of exercises. At the same time, seek out the company of people you can count on to help you shift perspectives, and avoid those who prefer to crawl around with you in each pit you slip into. What you are looking for are irritating, positive-minded pioneers who have wrangled their way out of the grip of fear and expect you to do the same.

Reframing the past. Your view of the past may be narrowing your perception of the present, making it harder to step into. By reframing the past, as described in figure 2–1, you can widen your current scope of possibilities.

Figure 2–1

A New Frame for Past Events

To live more fully in the present, place a new frame around difficult segments of your past by following these steps.

- Isolate a troublesome or painful piece of your past and mentally surround it with a frame, recalling the way you envisioned it at the time.

- Explore other reasons for the extenuating circumstances—possibilities you have never before considered.

- Replace the old frame with one of these reasons. If necessary, make it up.

- Repeat this exercise with other difficult pieces of your past.

To my amazement, new frames emerged on their own around two chunks of my past. One involved my father, who I was sure rejected me when I turned thirteen years old. I had quit playing sports and going on weekend family outings, thus ending our "play time" together. Talking together had never been a priority. And when I began to fill my free time with sex and drugs, my father seemed to disappear from my life. I decided he had cast me out.

Twelve years later—two days before he died—my father told me he blamed himself for the difficulties I faced as a teen. He never knew what to say. Instead of disliking me, he was sad and embarrassed. I felt grateful to see my dad in a different light. With the reframing of my teenage years, I was able to spend our final moments together just loving him.

The second reframing occurred long after my father died. My younger brother, who had taken over the family business, filed for bankruptcy. Soon afterward, my mother died and my brother inherited what was left of my father's estate, leaving nothing for me and our two siblings. He then sold the property. The money disappeared. Feeling cheated, I quit speaking to him since, from my point of view, he had deceived my mother and screwed my father. I could never forgive him for being so evil. Worse, I could not bear the thought of him caring so little about me.

A year later, I had dinner with an old friend who knew my family. I told him about my brother's actions. He replied, "Didn't you know your brother was a gambler?" In that moment, I forgave my brother. The behavior of an addict was something I could understand, having been down that road myself. Whether or not my friend was right, he shattered the judgment I had placed on my brother and, in the process, broke my frame. I was free to love him again.

No longer resentful, I was able to speak to my brother. Now when I am with him, I see the humanity in his eyes. He is not evil; he's a being who makes mistakes. I can see that he harbors anger and resentment of his own, as well as loneliness and confusion. Most important, he fears losing my love. Through reframing, I have been able to let go of the past and see in the present the possibility of a relationship.

Although you cannot change the past, you can change how you feel about it. Regrets, anger, blame, and confusion are minutes wasted. They drain your energy, reducing your ability to enjoy the present.

Redefining the present. Recasting the present, like reframing the past, provides an immediate pull into the here-and-now. A simple way to redefine it is by giving it new labels.

To do this, listen to the words you now use. For example, how many times a day do you say *can't* and *but?* According to the Talmud, an ancient Jewish book of wisdom for daily living, we do not see things as they are but rather as we are. If you feel unattractive, useless, or cheated, you'll see the world as a hostile dungeon with no way out. If you love yourself and trust that all things work out for the best, you'll find the hidden stairway back to the castle.

Iyanla Vanzant's advice is to "throw out your vocabulary," replacing the old staples with new words. She recommends changing, among other terms, the following:

Problem	to	Divine opportunity
Hard	to	Challenging
Single (in relationship)	to	Ready for the next experience
Broke	to	Temporarily out of cash
By myself	to	With myself
I'm afraid	to	I desire assistance and support

Changing your words will help shift your feelings and, as a result, your train of thought. Change your thoughts and you change your life.

I recently won a door prize at a meeting held by an organization whose board I sit on. While returning to my seat, I heard a woman mutter, "That was rigged." She was right. I had rigged the drawing. I've been rigging them for years—winning because I expect to win. Sometimes I hear my mind say, "I'll win that free trip." Then my number is called. Yet I can recall an earlier time when my mind would say, "I might as well leave. I never win anyway." When my mind changed its message, my luck changed, too.

How often do you tell yourself you are going to blow an event, and then proceed to do just that? Or do you focus on the worst, saying, "I can't get a cold now," or "What if I don't make enough money?" or "Please don't call on me," only to have your prophecies fulfilled? You, too, are a winner. Your prize is what you think about. You get the cold, your income falters, or you get called on with the hardest question. Your mind acts on the images it sees. It doesn't see "can't" or "don't." It only sees the pictures you paint.

So start with a clean canvas. Whether the storm of difficulties you are experiencing is an annoying sprinkle or a raging gale, avoid focusing on your losses. Instead, pursue the opportunities. Face each challenge. Anticipate the next one. Declare conditions temporary. Take time to be with yourself. Allow others to give you the gifts of assistance and support. Sing songs. Go dancing. Buy a Jana Stanfield CD.

Jana Stanfield writes delightful and profound lyrics that she puts to catchy, mind-sticking music. Her words can brighten any day and breathe air back into your faith. The chorus to one of her songs reads as follows:

I'm not lost,
I am exploring.
Life is an adventure worth enjoying.
Though I may not know where I'm going,
I am not lost, I am exploring.

Let Stanfield's lyrics remind you that the words you use to define yourself and your situation dictate the ease or difficulty of your transformation. Adversity can be strengthening rather than crippling.

Actor Christopher Reeve, paralyzed in a horseback riding accident, found a new career path. He is now a spokesman for people living with disabilities. His fame helps direct grant money to spinal cord injury research and treatment. As a result, doctors are on the brink of repairing damaged spinal cords. Reeve is helping others, and maybe himself, to walk again. The accident did not stop his life. It broadened his talents. And he has returned to his acting career.

FIGURE 2–2

Creating a Judgment-Free Zone

To redefine a present hardship you are facing, work with this practice daily. After one month, it is likely to lead to a good habit.

- Tell yourself, "For the next 10 minutes, I will not judge this situation as good or bad." Contain the fears. Slay the complaints. Suspend the blame or envy. Tell your misery to take a hike. Then proceed to do anything you wish. (If you slip before 10 minutes pass, start over.)

- The next day, repeat this procedure, extending the time to 20 minutes.

- The following day, strive to be judgment-free for 30 minutes.

- Continue to increase your practice until you can spend 60 minutes in the judgment-free zone.

Like Vanzant, Stanfield, and Reeve, you can define the present with words that liberate *your* soul. Find the words that help you feel strong. If you can't shift your perspective just yet, declare a moratorium and try the exercise in figure 2–2.

One reason I travel so much in my RV is that it gives me an opportunity to redefine my present many times a day regardless of what has been bothering me. Trips never go as planned. Roads are closed, rains slow me down, batteries die, reservations vanish, my cell phone goes on the blink, and my body complains. My greatest pleasures are a hot shower at the end of the day and some fresh, cooked food to eat somewhere nearby. I fall asleep grateful for these simple pleasures. Then I wake up to beautiful mountain views and greetings from the campground chipmunks.

If you see the present as a wild adventure, you too will handle the bumps with grace. Keep broadening your outlook. Rather than focus on what is missing, notice the beauty in the landscape, the fun in your work, and the richness in every soul you meet. For additional practice in breaking down judgments and seeing from different points of view, work with the game described in figure 2–3.

FIGURE 2–3

The Beliefs Game

To break out of the mold of your current perspective and see new options, follow these instructions. You will need a pen or pencil, a sheet of paper, and a friend.

- Identify a situation in which someone's actions are annoying, frustrating, disappointing, or hurtful to you.

- On the sheet of paper, state why you believe the person is treating you this way.

- Describe the situation to your friend. (Your friend can ask questions for clarification, but should not try to help you resolve the dilemma or determine who is right or wrong.)

When you have finished, make sure your friend understands how you see the situation.

- Read your belief statement to your friend, further clarifying what you think is at the root of the person's behavior.

- Tell your friend to adopt your belief.

- Spend 5 minutes arguing with your friend, finding ways to discount your original belief and exploring other reasons for the person's actions. Throughout the passionate debate, make sure neither you nor your friend gives in to the other's point of view.

- To summarize the insights you have gleaned, record your answers to these questions:

> What did you find out about your situation while examining it from a new perspective?

> Did you feel a shift in your emotions? If so, write a description of the change you experienced.

> What options do you now have in thinking about the situation, and in acting on it?

> What action, if any, will you take?

Repeat this game as often as you like, taking on a new perspective each time. The better you are at disconnecting from your beliefs, the sooner you will be prepared to shift your point of view. Do not let self-destructive beliefs guide your behavior.

COURAGE

Marcia Preston, in her essay "Spring Resolution," writes, "The first voice of spring on our acre [in Oklahoma] is a little brown wren about as long as my finger. In late winter, while the sun still shivers below the horizon, I hear him in the half-light, boldly advertising for a mate. Indoors, as I grope my way toward the computer, I wonder at his optimism. On his darkest day, he believes in spring."

Courage is a state of mind that depends heavily on faith. Laura Berman Fortgang, author of *Take Yourself to the Top,* encourages us to cultivate the "faith factor," and faith, she reminds us, is stronger than hope. Whereas hope is often based on a clinging need, faith relies on the ability to detach from knowing. Hope holds on to a rigid expectation. Faith yields to possibility. Hope is attached to fear. Faith is based on trust. With faith, you move open-mindedly, accepting that the twists and turns in the path are important to your journey. Meeting roadblocks with the confidence born of faith, you will succeed. Hope drains energy. Faith releases it.

In this context, faith is different from religious convictions, for it comes from the inside out. It starts with believing in yourself. Then it grows into trusting that there is lawful order in the universe. If you go with the flow, you will come to understand why events occur as they do. Your religion may support your faith, and vice versa.

For visible results, faith must be wedded to action. Napoleon Hill, author of *Think and Grow Rich*, said, "For it to be useful to you in achieving lasting success, it must be an active, not a passive, faith." An active faith sets wishes and dreams into motion. Step forward and the winds of change blow with you. Sit back and the air stagnates, letting wishes and dreams fall to the ground.

Therefore, to feel joy you must have the courage to act—with or without a clear picture of the outcome—and you must act when opportunities appear. If you say, "I desire to change my life, I'm willing, I see possibilities, but I don't feel like growing today," then the universal flow passes on to a more adventurous soul waiting around the corner. Someone else will take the job, create the product, write the story, trademark the business name, win the prospective partner. Opportunity is not likely to wait for you to get in gear.

What gives rise to the courage to act? It starts with claiming our personal powers. Start by being daring, devoted, enthusiastic, intelligent, savvy, tenacious, funny, patient, and caring, or however you defined your powers. Claim who you "be."

Mythologist Joseph Campbell advised us to discover the meaning of courage by looking at what makes a person a "hero." The journey all heroes take, he said, leads them on mysterious adventures and into fabulous battles, bringing them home with knowledge and rewards to share. Heroes call on their internal powers to stand strong before monsters. They clear their minds, casting out the urge to resist, fight, or flee. In the clearing, they access their greatest weapon—instinctual consciousness, or wisdom. Courage, in this sense, is the thread that weaves desire, willingness, and creativity into the structure of who you are. It promotes a feeling of wholeness, integrating aspects of yourself that have been contrary to your nature, transforming you into someone new as you take on the trials of life.

To inspire your courage, try the freeze-frame technique described below. While relieving worry, anxiety, and frustration, it helps pave the way to action. If you begin by practicing this exercise in relatively unchallenging moments, it is likely to bear fruit in more heated ones, when concentration may be difficult.

FIGURE 2–3

The Freeze-Frame Technique

To muster up the courage to act once you have said "no" to trying something new, follow these steps.

• Imagine seeing yourself in a video. You are resistant to doing something you know you need to do.

• Hit the pause button.

• Ask the frozen image of yourself the following questions: If, as a hero, you had the courage to move forward, what would it feel like? What actions would you take?

• Release the pause button and listen to the answers.

• Reengaging the pause button, ask the image: What might the possible consequences be? Will you die? Will you lose a limb? Will you lose your job? Will you lose a loved one? If you won't be seriously impacted, is living a joyous life worth risking the possible consequences?

• Release the pause button and listen to the answers.

- Hit the pause button and ask the image of yourself to play out the next scene in this movie. If you act on your desire, what will happen? In the story of your life, how does this scene end?

- Releasing the pause button, watch the actions you perform and the outcomes they produce. If the results look appealing, or at least nonthreatening, you may safely assume that you are capable of performing such acts of bravery today.

The freeze-frame technique invites us to go into our hearts and listen for answers. "As a man thinketh in his heart, so he is," the Bible tells us. And experience teaches us that the more accustomed we are to taking risks, the more adept we are at bouncing back to our feet.

Sometimes I do the freeze-frame exercise while scheduling threatening events into my DayTimer. Then when it comes time to act, I punch in the phone number, make the major purchase, take the day off, get a commitment to meet for that much-needed conversation, start my next book, pack up my old books, or take the first step into the next chapter of my life.

Always, we need to wipe the brain clean in order to hear what the heart has to say. And so we take frequent rests stops, finding quiet moments to reflect. As the Buddha put it, "To be happy, rest like a great tree in the midst of it all."

When the storms hit, large or small, go to a quiet place where you can clear your mind long enough to hear the whispers of your love, laughter, and dreams. The moment the mind is empty, joy finds a way to shine through. Using this light, claim your desires, declare your willingness, create possibilities, and boldly leap over the puddles the rain left behind.

Part II

VENTURING INTO THE VERTICAL WORLD

If you choose the road less traveled,
be sure to take your four-wheel drive.

—Marcia Reynolds

While planning a trip up the California coast, I visited our local American Automobile Association (AAA) to pick up a map. I walked out with a personalized Triptik, a spiral-bound set of maps outlining my journey. The Triptik highlighted the most direct route, along with scenic back-roads and places of interest along the way. It also indicated current construction spots and areas where driving might be hazardous. My conversation with the AAA agent lasted an hour longer than the ten minutes I'd estimated. She strove to understand my wants and needs—my picture of a perfect trip. Then she pointed out simpler alternatives to the course I'd chosen. Together, we planned the most pleasurable adventure for me.

Preparations are much the same for venturing into the vertical world of rapture. Confident and ready to create a life of our dreams, we choose our destination based on our purpose; envision our map, including how to negotiate the byways and detours; and decide how and when to reach particular milestones. Finally, map in hand, we take the leap, trusting that we are equipped to handle the bumps and surprises along the way.

Alice, upon meeting the Cheshire Cat at the fork in the road in Lewis Carroll's *Alice's Adventures in Wonderland,* asks, "Would you tell me, please, which way I ought to go from here?"

"That depends a good deal on where you want to get to," says the Cat.

"I don't much care where as long as I get somewhere."

"Then it doesn't matter which way you go."

Without a clear sense of direction, your journey may be like Alice's, punctuated with detours and dark passageways. If instead you take the time to lay out a plan, you'll be able to step out of your head and participate fully in the adventure called living, all the while trusting that you've made the right choices.

Of course, any day you might wake up and decide to alter your plan. A new purpose may arise. An insight could change your vision. Such modifications are easy, because there's no absolute set of goals to adhere to. You'll be living life, not collecting achievements. You'll be free to respond to circumstances, rather than trapped in a struggle. Guided by your purpose and vision, you will be at liberty to travel wherever you wish.

The next five chapters will help you design a Triptik for navigating the vertical world. Less detailed than AAA's, it will allow for greater variation in accessing your destination. You'll begin by practicing presence, a discipline that opens portals to the vertical world. Next, you'll have a chance to clarify your purpose and formulate a vision and methods for manifesting it—all of which will define the coordinates of your path. Then, since the trip itself will always be a mystery, you'll find tips to help with decision making.

Free to roam while camping in the woods, I love to take morning hikes. I start by reminding myself to pay attention to the path so I can find my way back. Soon the sun peeks over the horizon, clouds burst to life in pinks and oranges, and birds beckon me to follow them. Usually, by the time my stomach insists on a return for breakfast, I've lost sight of the familiar landmarks. My breath shortens, my heart pounds, and my pace quickens. Then I slow down and release the doubts that have been running rampant. I know I'll find my way back. I always do. The homeward trek might take an hour longer than I've calculated, but since I know the direction of the campsite, it eventually comes into view.

Why do I continue to get lost? Perhaps to test my sense of trust. Each time I feel afraid or frustrated, I remember that as long as I know where I'm headed—well aware of my purpose and vision—things turn out for the best, often better. Knowing where I want to end up sooner or later brings me home.

With our hearts set on an intention, and our thoughts and actions aligned in manifesting a purpose, we are free to explore with less fear. Our encounters, even if different from what we expected, turn out to be just what we've asked for. While moving through the vertical world, the euphoria we feel has less to do with achievements and accomplishments than with the satisfaction of knowing we are on the right road. Life feels lighter as we glide through the adventure.

CHAPTER 3

Zoning In

Anything worth doing
is worth doing effortlessly.

—Les Fehmi

While wandering with a friend through an Oregon campground, I watched a mother order her young daughter to be quiet. The little girl was lost in a talkative game of make-believe, taking guidance from a tree wizard on how to act like a bear. My friend and I bet on how long it would take this child to lose her creativity, to have her passion doused by her mother's rules.

Joy is an involuntary experience. All we do is clear a space, both inwardly and outwardly, for it to happen. Then we allow ourselves to "free fall" into the moment. Actions are effortless, flowing, and instinctive. Time ceases to exist. Behavior is responsive, not forceful or needy. The imagination opens up. In essence, we recapture our capacity for child's play.

The natural spontaneity of childhood is often quelled early in life. Schools replace crayons with sharp pencils. Teachers bestow awards for staying in line, writing within lines, imitating proper behavior, and reiterating correct words. Many children who remain in tune with their creativity find ways to manipulate the system. They strive for good grades with the least amount of study. Or they form small cliques, discounting as inferior anyone who doesn't "get" who they are. More rebellious children are penalized—something they continue to pay for as adults.

While sorting through old family papers after my mother died, I found my elementary school report cards. I had earned all A's and B's. Yet my first six teachers wrote critical remarks. They claimed I had a social problem—I talked excessively, failed to apply myself, and worked too hard for the attention of my peers. I remember standing in corners wearing tape over my mouth and being repeatedly sent to the end of the lunch line. What was my greatest faux pas? I "played" and "laughed" at inappropriate times.

Fortunately, my joy was saved by my sixth grade teacher, Miss Wickware. Her only comment on my report card was, "Doesn't she just love everyone!" Instead of punishing me for talking, Miss Wickware moved my desk next to hers. When she wasn't teaching, she let me blab to my heart's content. If I tried to be funny while she was leading class, she lightly teased me. I'd back down without feeling bad. Mostly I behaved well, not wanting to upset her. I learned more that year than in all previous years combined. And my self-esteem soared.

Subsequent teachers had no patience for my antics, despite the good grades. I was expelled from classes. I rebelled. Angry, I eventually did lose the sense of play they were trying to wean me of. Robbed of passion, it took me nearly two decades to recover it.

Once squelched, spontaneity is not easily accessed after childhood. One reason is that our culture frowns on a return to childhood and equates "childlike" with the pejorative "childish." Acting *childish*, implying neglect or ignorance, can bring harm to oneself, others, or the environment. Being *childlike*—silly or whimsical—frees us to embrace more of life. In fact, the childlike capacity for play is our greatest defense amid arduous challenges.

Another reason playfulness is difficult to recapture is that it's often deeply suppressed. Early on, we learned that toddlers at play are considered innocent and creative whereas adolescents and adults at play are viewed as irresponsible and frivolous. To avoid negative labels while growing up, we conformed to expectations, allowing our fears to override our pleasures. Rather than doing what we loved, we bogged ourselves down with questions: "What will people think?" "Am I dressed correctly (behaving properly, saying the right thing)?" "Will I make my point (earn their respect, be treated as if I'm important)?" The mind's endless chatter succeeded in burying spontaneity.

How do we relearn the fine art of playing? Some people tackle this question by studying the behavior of young animals and children. I took a different route: I researched the habits of top athletes and performers. Play, I discovered, need not be foolish. It can be directed and productive. Play, in these terms, is a mental state that overrules the brain and transforms the body into a vehicle of focused, inspired energy. Athletes refer to this state as being "in the zone."

THE ZONE AS A STATE OF BEING

Five years ago, a television reporter asked to interview me on the "zone of performance." Her theory was that the zone referred to by athletes was accessible through all activities and that anyone could reach a peak of excellence. She had already interviewed several well-known athletes and artists. Although they agreed that being in the zone is the epitome of performance, they could not describe how to get there. The reporter suspected that the steps I used in coaching could provide the missing link, adding credence to her theory.

To prepare for the interview, I pored over books, articles, and interviews with champions. I found similarities among what athletes do to prepare for entering the zone. And sure enough, their methods corresponded to many of the techniques I taught my clients.

However, when the camera flashed on, the interviewer's first question was, "Please define how it feels to be in the zone." Unprepared to address the emotions involved, I had no idea what to say. Immediately, my mind flashed on the last time I had been in the zone. I was leading a workshop, and the participants were so responsive that I jumped in, freely sharing and interacting with them. Rather than try to figure out what they were thinking, I trusted my wisdom and acted on my gut instincts. They, in turn, offered ideas, challenged concepts, laughed, clapped, and cheered me on. Seeing them palpably shift their perspectives energized me even more. Insights seemed to come at me straight from the universe, shooting through my brain and out my mouth. The room practically vibrated!

"The zone," I told the reporter, "is a place of total immersion, erasing all differences between a person and their performance. 'Doing' slips away until there is only 'being.' The mind is so clear that it acts like a perfect conduit for wisdom coming from elsewhere. Time stands still. The world exists only in the moment."

I was unhappy with my response. It was too intellectual. It hardly touched on the depth of pleasure I'd experienced at the workshop. But the reporter had moved on.

Her next question veered the conversation toward what people have to do to get to the zone. I gave her four action steps. Then the session ended.

Three months later, determined to better articulate my experience of the vertical world and how to get there, I produced an audiotape titled *Being in the Zone: The Secrets of Performance Excellence*. Listeners sent me mail describing career successes they achieved after listening to the tape. Then, a man wrote to say that practicing the steps daily had transformed his *life*. He felt happier, often ecstatic, and his marriage had vastly improved. I began to wonder if the action steps could extend beyond achieving goals to enriching one's experience of life.

Returning to my stacks of research, I found that many athletes had described the zone as exhilarating. Few spoke of winning. Most recounted an experience of joy well before the outcome, suggesting that peak performance was a side effect. They rode in on passion and bliss. I concluded that lasting happiness could indeed be found by following the steps for achieving peak performance. If applied to day-to-day realities, the steps could certainly help people learn how to live in the zone. Here was a path into the world of being that felt as free as child's play. In looking for what it takes to perform at a level of excellence, I had broken through the doorway to spontaneity and joy.

DESCRIPTIONS OF LIFE IN THE ZONE
Champions describe their experiences of the zone in ecstatic terms. In his book *Ski Extreme*, skier Patrick Vallencant writes, "At the beginning of any steep descent, concentration of incredible intensity fills me. . . . When I concentrate so, the world disappears." Olympic medalist Gary Hall Jr. says he feels "a burst of excitement, adrenaline. It's 100%

pure rush." Throwing a touchdown pass, according to football star Joe Namath, is "an incredible feeling. It's like your whole body's bursting with happiness." Mountain climber Robert Schaller observes, "[Climbing is] like a child running free through a candy store. The feel of the trail under my feet, the smell of the wilderness, watching the ever-changing cloud patterns . . . everything suddenly has more meaning." Tennis star Billie Jean King speaks of feeling "transported above the turmoil." The body, freed of thoughts, merges with the moment. Body, mind, and universe melt into one.

In their book *In the Zone*, researchers Michael Murphy and Rhea White show that dedicated athletes deeply explore their inner realities, setting foot in spiritual territories most people never enter. They conclude, "Sport has an enormous power to sweep us beyond our ordinary sense of self, to evoke capacities that have generally been regarded as mystical, occult, or religious." Most athletes would not characterize this phenomenon as religious. Yet once they feel the exhilaration it brings, they actively attempt to repeat the experience.

You, too, have the capacity to live in the moment any time you want to—on the job or while tinkering with a hobby in your backyard. You can feel the excitement of the zone while surrounded by people or off on your own, while harmonizing with a choir or writing a software program, while out with friends or nestled at home with your lover. You can even glide into the zone while shuttling your children to and from school, racing to a meeting, paying your bills, or washing the car.

Following are firsthand accounts from three people who have entered this vertical dimension from different walks of life. Josie, a factory worker who has been making semiconductor chips for more than fourteen years, says: "There are days when I'm so in the flow, nothing in my area can go wrong and no one can bother me. There's a rhythm I get into. It feels like the pulse of life. I go home at the end of the day feeling more energy than when I woke up."

Tom, recalling a marketing meeting during his first year as president of a large corporation, notes: "After falling miserably on my face for months, I stood up that day and—*pow!*—I hit the jackpot. I gave up caring what they thought. Just laid out my plan. I worked hard. Knew it was good. I slipped into the moment where everything I said was perfect. There was silence. Then applause. From that day on, I had the support I needed to succeed."

Janice runs a small tailoring business from her home while raising three school-age children. She explains: "I love to sing. The kids have learned to sing with me—in the car and while cleaning the house. I feel a little like Mary Poppins, but it beats getting angry and stressed."

You have probably known similar moments. To recall the feelings you had while in the zone, try this exercise.

FIGURE 3–1

Recapturing a Moment in the Zone

Emotions experienced in the zone are forever available to you. You can replay the memory any time you wish by following these instructions.

- Think back to a time when you were having so much fun that nothing else mattered. Perhaps you were building a model, writing a letter, or sharing memories with a long-time friend. Or maybe you were hiking, cooking, or taking part in a play.
- Mentally, reenact the memory. Recall the setting. Connect with the moment. In your imagination, acquiesce to your body's movements and the words you were speaking. Perform at your best. Delight in yourself. Feel your heart swell with vitality and gratitude.

The zone state of mind, even if entered only once, can be life altering. Marty, a purchasing department employee and MBA student, is convinced that being in the zone while umping a Little League team has changed his life. His wife and his manager often remark on his increased energy and happiness.

Whether you are officiating from behind home plate or sipping tea at sunset, while in the zone state you don't focus on doing anything. You are in a sacred space where "no things" exist. Your mind is clear of thoughts about the past and future, your body is moving with effortless ease, and your heart is taking in the beauty of the moment. This space is vibrant with possibility. It's the source of human potential. Released from frustration, anxiety, and ambition, you're left with the grace of a child and the courage of a hero. No longer "thinking things through" or "making them happen," you are simply being.

Who do you want to be? A loving, compassionate, happy person? An industrious, committed, playful person? Who do you want to be *just for today?* Focus on being that person and see how freeing it is. When you are busy being, the "doing" is less frustrating, and often fun.

Sound easy? It's as easy as changing careers or moving a family halfway around the world. The reason it's so challenging to "zone in" is that we have spent a lifetime mastering "zoning out." As a result, we are experts at juggling today's tasks while planning tomorrow's. We're proficient at guessing what other people are thinking and at calculating their reactions. Girls learn early on how to assess paternal approval. Boys discover the rewards of winning. Our minds are forever either balancing opinions across space or moving back and forth through time. Little energy is devoted to the here-and-now.

Consider, for instance, how good you are at multitasking. When someone is speaking to you, can you look them in the eye, nod, smile, acknowledge their statements with "uh-huh" and "I see" while silently deciding where to go for lunch? Can you formulate a plan, create a dinner menu, and mentally list your weekend tasks while listening to a friend's confidences? If so, this talent must really shine when you are on the phone. While conversing, you are probably able to *write* the plan, *cook* dinner, and *complete* the chores. For many people, it takes sitting in front of a television set or staring at a computer to stop their minds from multitasking. Even then, worries and unfinished work often creep into the crevices of the brain, pulling them away from the present.

Few of us know how to taste the sweetness of the moment. Even fewer know how to savor this pleasure over time. Yet both experiences are within reach. You have mastered the ability to accomplish many goals at once. Surely you can learn to corral your mind into paying attention to what is happening now.

FROM ZONING OUT TO ZONING IN

Long-time preoccupations with the horizontal world have contributed to deeply embedded mental habits. Shaking them loose in order to play again, traveling freely into the vertical world of the zone, often takes a bit of work. A good way to start is by learning to hold your attention in the present through *active meditation*.

Contrary to popular opinion in most Western cultures, meditation need not be practiced with closed eyes in a quiet corner. A form of practice known as *active meditation*, described in figure 3–2, can in fact be used for focusing in the midst of a busy day. Meditation in this sense is a fine-tuning tool. It helps us tune out distractions so that we can fully tune in to one thought or one sensation. It lets us take control of our mental state by consciously choosing what will enter our brain and what will not, expanding our capacity to see more of what is in front of us. As if your mind were a camera, you set it on "wide-angle view." Colors intensify. Details enlarge. Information increases. Your reactions quicken. Your outlook broadens.

Active meditation can even help you create a more satisfying present. You step into the moment and alternatives appear. You choose those you would like to focus on. You discover new meaning behind uncomfortable situations. You uncover dormant seeds of joy in your sadness or frustration. Tended to, they sprout blossoms. No matter how muddy circumstances may appear in the horizontal world, the present moment holds secrets for maneuvering through them. If you choose to, you can live your life in active meditation.

FIGURE 3–2

Active Meditation

Practice this exercise for 20 minutes at least once a day. After two weeks, plan to transfer your practice to new settings. Before long, you will know what it feels like to live in active meditation.

- **Find a time and place where you can be alone.** Early morning, late at night, or between tasks will work well. Give yourself the

---

gift of seclusion in a corner of the library; in your car, the garden, or a tree; or at your desk. If you are at home with children, declare a personal time-out and retreat to a quiet spot, setting an alarm to let them know when you'll return. If your day is booked, arrive early for an appointment.

- **Remove outer distractions.** Turn off the television, unplug the phone, and close the front door. Hide all reading material, including junk mail and the cereal box you've read forty times. Set the thermostat at a comfortable temperature or arrange your clothing so that you are neither too warm nor too chilly. Then sit down and breathe comfortably to relax.

- **Clear out inner distractions.** Slowly count to 10, relieving yourself of "should dos" and other messages. If a thought begins to run through your head, focus on it for 2 minutes, replaying the words in your mind until you tire of them. Then free the thought for the rest of the session—or better yet, for good. Remind yourself that you chose this moment to practice attentiveness. You don't need to be anywhere else. Twenty minutes will pass soon enough.

- **Focus on a 4- by 4-foot area in front of you.** For the remainder of your session, discover every possible detail in your environment. Look for specks of dust. Notice patterns on the ground, or on your dashboard or desk. Feel the density and texture of the surface beneath you. Touch the objects within your reach. While looking at objects that are in direct sunlight, squint your eyes. See glass sparkle. Look for scratches in plastic. Smell scents in the air. Is the wind blowing? Concentrate on sounds. Do you hear machinery, cars, or people? How about birds, leaves, or bugs?

- **After 15 minutes, conduct a body scan.** Are wisps of hair touching your ear? Does you mouth feel fresh or stale? Are your eyes energized or tired? Mentally, move into your chest and arms. Is your breathing deep or shallow? Are you sitting straight or slouched? Stroke your skin. Notice how your stomach feels. Become aware of how you are holding your feet. Now flex your muscles. Wiggle your fingers and toes. Stretch like a cat. Then reach for the sky and smile.

- If you've quit early, acknowledge the amount of time you gave yourself to be present and plan on a longer session tomorrow. If you've practiced overtime, thank yourself for being so kind.

After two weeks of 20-minute practice sessions, begin to transfer this meditation to your daily activities, one at a time. For example, while walking indoors or out, feel how differently your feet respond to tile, linoleum, dirt, rocks, grass, concrete, and asphalt. Walk toe first, then heel first. Alternate your steps from light to heavy. Speed up your pace and slow it down. Notice the movement of your arms, head, and jaw. Observe wall decor, furniture arrangements, birds, clouds, architecture, store windows, human interactions, and solitary individuals. Feel the wind or stillness in the air. Note changes in temperature. Feel your presence as you move. Assess each part of your body, how it functions and serves you. Command each space you enter. Walk slouched and walk tall. Own your world so that you can share it with others. Storm ahead, then let yourself flow with the current of the universe.

Also bring active meditation to your driving—especially during rush hour, while inching along in traffic. Using all your senses, pay attention to the interior of the car, traffic patterns, the timing of stoplights, the landscape, where birds are perched, the condition of the road, the progress of construction sites, the onset of destruction, and the facial expressions of other drivers. Leaving the radio off, watch the changing scenes as if they were movie segments. All the while, exercise caution. Keeping a wide-angle view, remain aware of everything that is happening around you.

Gradually transfer your daily practice to your work, recreation, and interactions with others. Be mindful of what you are doing and who you are with. Notice the details. The more awareness you bring to the present moment, the sooner you'll experience joy. Even tasks you consider mundane can take on a delightful quality when performed with total immersion. For now, practice attentiveness one day at a time. Before long, you'll be in the grip of a pleasant habit.

What if the present moment is unbearable—your job is insufferable, your home life a nightmare, or your primary relationship hurtful? By cultivating the desire, willingness, creativity, and courage discussed in chapter 2, you can begin to see the circumstances in a new light. Recognize your lessons. Notice possibilities for growth. Observe the fear behind someone's hurtful words, then practice compassion. Seize the chance to choose love over anger. Find an opportunity to take back control of your life, if only to take charge of your thoughts. To further increase your capacity to step out of your head and into the zone, give yourself extra doses of faith and patience.

Understand that people living under extremely oppressive circumstances experience moments of ecstasy. In fact, studies show that survivors of concentration camps, people in chronic physical pain, and populations exposed to hostile weather conditions exhibit similar sustaining mechanisms. First, they learn how to order their thoughts. Second, they either redefine their reality or soothe their minds through an activity such as singing, writing, or helping the disadvantaged. Together, these endeavors tip the scales of thought from negative to positive.

To stay in this realm of pleasure, such people anchor themselves to a strong purpose and choose the content that enters their minds, rather than allow themselves to be run over by uncontrollable thoughts of dire consequences. Purpose, according to psychiatrist and Holocaust survivor Victor Frankl, is the element that kept concentration camp prisoners alive. The sustaining capacity of perspective is extolled by Mihaly Csikszentmihalyi, author of *Flow: The Psychology of Optimal Experience*, who notes, "In conditions of extreme deprivation poets, mathematicians, musicians, historians, and biblical experts have stood out as islands of sanity surrounded by waves of chaos."

Purpose and perspective saved my life, too, when I sank into deep despair in jail. From the moment I chose to take back control of my existence, beginning with my physical body and extending into a desire to help others, I regained my voice. I wrote with renewed passion, sang my favorite tunes, and delighted in my cellmates' laughter. Having a purpose turned the light back on. My renewed perspective kept it shining. Even while behind bars, I was able to experience sustained moments in the zone.

Regardless of your circumstances recognize, as you work with the steps in the next four chapters, that creating a new way to be takes time. You need time to reflect, make choices, clear your life of fears and useless needs, and get used to the new you. So be gentle with yourself. Remain confident. Remind yourself of how powerful you already are. Then release your need for perfection. Remember, you're relearning how to play. The more you relax and have fun, the sooner the magic will appear.

Simply practice one step at a time. As you practice, you become.

CHAPTER 4

Living Life "On Purpose"

I survived . . .
by dreaming that someday
I'd be speaking about
how I survived.

—Victor Frankl

I remember the day I chose to live. It was soon after I went to jail. Yet it was before I met Vicki, who helped me feel the power to re-create my life. Days earlier, I'd determined that I had a purpose for living.

Upon entering jail as a nineteen-year-old heroin addict, I was devoid of possessions and desires. I vowed to do my time peacefully. I wanted no trouble. I prayed for no pain. I did my best to be invisible.

However, loneliness found a way of seeping into my bones. And boredom edged out my thoughts. Soon I was talking to anyone within earshot. To my surprise and gratitude, cellmates I had feared transformed into friends.

One day, my cellmate Carmella received news that her brother had committed suicide. She shrieked. Two of us tried to console her. We wanted to relieve her pain. We also wanted to avoid a scene with the guards. I begged her to stop screaming. She ignored me. I tried to make her laugh. Nothing worked. Exasperated, I grabbed her in a bear hug. She shoved me to the floor, flung herself against the bars, and hollered obscenities at God and the world.

Within seconds, our cell filled with guards attacking, arms flying, scuffling, slapping, kicking, and screams. Thinking I heard Carmella call my name, I instinctively launched into action. I jumped on the back of a guard. He flung me to the ground. I rose up. Another guard rushed toward me. Headfirst, he rammed into my stomach. I crashed into the wall. Flipping me out the door, he locked his arms around my elbows. I twisted, kicked, and tried to pull away. He dragged me down the hall.

When we reached the dayroom, he threw me inside. I curled up to soften the fall. The door slammed behind me.

Silence. It was over, quick and stinging like a slap in the face. No words. No reasons. Tossed aside and left for dead.

I dragged myself to a corner. Propping myself up between the adjacent walls, I hugged my thighs to my chest and dropped my head to my knees.

"Please, God, let me die," I pleaded silently, my eyes burning. The stench of sweat clogged my nose. I opened my mouth but could push no sounds out of my throat. My head throbbed. My heart shut down. No anger. No sorrow. I was blank—a hollow shell. Even my breathing was silent.

As I drifted off to sleep, an old melody about butterflies flying free reached my ears. Then an image of butterflies in the field behind my father's warehouse floated through my mind. The field was wild with flowering yellow weeds. I was six years old and had just started school. Wearing a pin I'd earned as the week's best reader, I eagerly displayed my trophy to the bees and other insects. How smart I felt. How lucky. I danced as if my legs had wings. Then I ran as fast as I could, licking the wind as I laughed out loud.

A door slammed, jolting me awake. No one was there. Hearing the music, I traced its source to the speakers mounted in the catwalk. I remembered that the night shift sometimes played the radio to lull us to sleep. The graceful yet passionate voice sang, "Someone saved my life tonight."

I stood. Shaking, I made my way to the center of the room, eyes fixed on the thin steel columns that kept me from the outside world.

The phrase "sweet freedom" drifted into my ears, then "You're a butterfly. And butterflies are free to fly..."

"Let me go," I said, my voice strained but audible.

"Fly away, high away, bye-bye."

I reached through the bars, raised a fist to the ceiling, and cried out, "It's my life." The word *life* echoed down the catwalk. My voice strengthened. Pressing my face against the cold steel, I could see a ray of light sift through the window at the end of the hall. Somewhere beyond, wildflowers beckoned. Butterflies fluttered gaily toward the sun.

I stepped back and lifted my dress. My skin was pale, my stomach swollen. Yet my legs were still strong. Strong enough to carry me on a long-distance run.

Lying on the cement, I stretched my legs over a bench and tucked my hands beneath my head. I breathed in deeply, then exhaled as I touched elbows to knees. "One...two...three...."

I worked past the quivering and cramping, counting thirty sit-ups. I rolled over for push-ups. Then jumping jacks. I ran in place, slapping hands to knees, calling my count out loud. Stumbling and cursing, I pressed on. An inner fire raged, giving me unimaginable strength. I had to keep going. My life was waiting for me.

From there, the battle was uphill. I survived jail, beat my addiction, and moved toward a successful future. Yet most of the women I lived with those long months never made it. They returned to drugs and prostitution. Most wound up in prison—a fate that would have been mine as well had something not clicked that night in the dayroom.

What was it that pushed me over the line and drove me to fight back? Why does one person's will flourish in confinement while another's shrivels? Why does one factory worker strive for improvement and another succumb to frustration? Why does one cancer patient see the light of hope and another resign to die? Why did my dad, upon retiring, give up on living and my friend's father find new interests to fill his days? Most people who face a challenge and come out on the winning side do so because they discover a purpose to their lives and seize it.

We can feel happiness without knowing our purpose. Yet knowing it, even if the purpose is apt to change over time, we achieve so much more. Purpose helps us access profound pleasure at will rather than by accident. It motivates us to persist. When we live life "on purpose," our visions brighten, our dreams come true, and we are given fuel for living as the going gets tough. In the words of philosopher Friedrich Wilhelm Nietzsche, "He who has a why to live can bear with most any how."

Without a life purpose, it's easy to feel lost, overworked, unappreciated, and insignificant. Our thoughts dwell on escaping the present. With a purpose, we can barely sit still. Barbara Sher, a therapist and best-selling author, says that a purpose helps shape vague yearnings into an intentional adventure. For many people grappling with depression, she proposes, the solution is not therapy as much as it is a reason to get out of bed in the morning. If you feel passionate about your choices in life, she writes in her book *Wishcraft*, "you wake up every morning excited about the day ahead and delighted to be doing what you're doing, even if you're sometimes a little nervous and scared."

FINDING YOUR PURPOSE

At any given moment, we all have a purpose. Our task is simply to find it. We don't have to *create* a reason for being. Rather, we do what it takes to allow our purpose to reveal itself. Often, it shows up when we replace the age-old question "What is the meaning of life?" with "What is the meaning of *my* life at *this moment?*"

If an answer arises when you ponder this question, you can safely assume it points to the gift you came to share at this juncture in time. Try not to judge it as good or bad. A purpose can be as altruistic as finding a cure for AIDS or as personal as raising a child. It can be as enduring as a ministry or as temporary as rebuilding a business. You may be driven to write your memoirs or to share your musical talents. You may see your life as a testimony to the glory of God or seek health and vitality as a testament to life. You could focus your energy on finding spiritual answers or on inventing gadgets to facilitate earthly existence. Maybe you see yourself as a bearer of laughter in a gloomy workplace, or a storyteller intent on teaching lessons or offering promise. Your light might shine on many or warm a single soul, be it the soul of a person, an animal, or an old shade tree. One purpose is no better than another.

Whether you are here to be a civic leader, a firefighter, an entertainer, a marital partner, or an engineer—or all five at once—your purpose will infuse you with the sense that life is worth living.

Reporters recently documented the story of a man who, diagnosed with cancer, was told he had six months to live. Hearing the news, he replied, "Sorry to disagree with you, Doc, but I'll tell you how much time I have. One day longer than my wife. I love her too much to leave the planet without her." He lived another eighteen years—one year longer than his wife. The doctors declared him a walking miracle. When asked how he had far exceeded all expectations, he explained that as a medic during World War I, he had seen many amputated arms and legs—none of which worked on its own. So he decided he could tell his body parts how to behave. He stood up in obvious pain, looked at his chest, and said, "Shut up! We're having a party here." This man's purpose of lifelong partnership had given him control over his longevity.

Whereas for some people purpose is lifelong, for others it can change over time. At the moment I decided to fight for my life, my purpose was to take back control and achieve freedom. As I traversed that path, a new purpose emerged. Having found the power to rise above my circumstances, I decided to take others with me—to be a light of hope for them, whether they were incarcerated in a physical jail or in their own mental cells. Who knows what might be next.

Many times, purpose will change in response to maturity's broadening perspective. We often discover, for instance, that what we once considered our life's purpose was actually an expectation imposed by family, friends, or society. Once we strengthen our foundation, clear out the rubble left from fears and needs, and begin to honor our physical, emotional, and spiritual well-being, we find our true love. Then we begin to live the rest of our lives *on purpose*.

In seeking the purpose of your life at this moment, you will therefore want to disregard anything that resembles an obligation. A life purpose is never sacrificial. On the contrary, while pursuing activities that give you meaning, you should feel as if you are nourishing yourself. Any commitment—to stay with a job, a course of education, or a marriage—should help you feel as though you are fleshing out your plan. Ultimately, your purpose can serve as a benchmark for decision making, helping you veer away from rationalizing or from taking on what someone else says you "should do." When you consult with your heart, purposeful decisions feel right.

A sure sign that you are living your purpose is an abiding love for your endeavors. If you love persuading lawmakers to change the penal system, your purpose may be political advocacy. If you love writing poetry, your purpose may be to compose with words. If you love caring for an ailing relative, you may find meaning in caregiving. If you are engaging in these activities *without* passion, then your purpose lies elsewhere—most likely, beneath the surface of your day-to-day activities.

The passion that bubbles up as you find and further your true purpose will help you sustain extreme loss, great fears, and everyday doldrums. For this reason alone, discovering your mission is worth every ounce of attention you can give it.

Homing In on Your Purpose

In her book *Women Who Run with the Wolves,* Clarissa Pinkola Estés, PhD, refers to self-discovery as "homing." Dr. Estés says that during childhood we are in tune with our natural and soulful selves. Then time passes and circumstances rob us of what we perceive as a "great opportunity." Many adults speak of having lost the love of their life, having blown a chance at the "big time," or having made a decision that cost them their happiness. Stolen forever is their art, their dream, their belief in goodness, their humor, and their will to strive. In essence, they have forfeited their sense of self and their passion for living.

Dr. Estés goes on to say that although adults typically live in this state of psychic slumber, the psyche can be aroused through homing, or going home. Homing, in this context, has nothing to do with returning to the house you grew up in. Home is inside you, and homing has you looking in your heart for answers. There you will receive a "thumbs up" in response to pertinent questions you pose about your purpose in life.

To begin to find your way home, work with the exercise that appears on the following two pages. If your heart gives you a sense of your life's purpose, do what you can to embrace it. And welcome back your passion for living.

If instead you experience only a vague sense that something within you has shifted, give it time to come to awareness. For example, after considering question 14 and thinking about what drove your passion when

FIGURE 4–1

Going Home

Prepare to direct the divining rod of your awareness to yourself. During this exercise, your mind will be alive with pictures. Refrain from analyzing whether they are right or wrong. Insights don't come to a mind locked in judgment. Also, be patient. An answer may arise only after your memory has had a chance to play itself out in your conscious life, perhaps partway through the coming week. Finally, trust yourself. Allow images to flow freely through your mind, whether or not they make sense.

- Sit comfortably in a quiet, secluded spot—preferably out-doors—with paper and pen, or a tape recorder.

- Relax, and detach all thoughts from your mind. As thoughts enter that are unrelated to this exercise, ask them to leave for now.

- Ask yourself some or all of the following questions. Draw them into your heart, which may have been safeguarding ideas for many years, and record the first answers that come to mind. Then take time to contemplate your replies.

    1. What activities bring you the most pleasure?

    2. What do you do that brings pleasure to others?

    3. When and why do people seek you out?

    4. Do you like helping others relieve pain, seek out love, find happiness, feel safe, or express their creativity?

    5. What fires you up (as opposed to burning you out)?

    6. If you could live your most perfect day, how would you spend the majority of your time? What would you do the next day? After a month of these days, how would you spend the rest of the year?

7. If you could spend an entire day with any person, alive or dead, who would it be? Why? What do you most admire about this person?

8. If you could choose your life's work, assured that it would generate money and respect, what would it be? How would this line of work benefit you and others? (Remember, improving the quality of life for your family is as worthy as more altruistic charitable intentions.)

9. If you could teach all the children in the world one lesson, what would it be?

10. If you had your life to live over, what would you change? Why?

11. If you had your life to live over, what would you not change? Why?

12. Name two situations in your life that you regret and have chosen never to think about. What did they tell you about yourself? How might you use this knowledge to help someone else?

13. As you look back on your life, what recurring patterns do you see? What is their significance? How might you share this wisdom with others?

14. Find an instance in childhood or early adulthood when you were robbed of your happiness. (Consider parental or societal injunctions, as well as times involving a lack of money, time, or courage to go after what you wanted.) Reflecting on this loss, restructure the incident, changing the people, their actions, or the setting in order to take the chance. What would your life look like now if you had lived this moment in keeping with your script?

15. If you were the hero of a fairy tale, what would you be like? How would you spend your time? Who would your enemies be, and why? What would you do to get rid of them? Freed of these enemies, what would you do in the happily-ever-after?

you were younger, you may receive an answer while roaming through a hardware store. As you reach for a nail, the memory of sawing and hammering with your father might flood your mind as if released from a dam, reminding you of your love for creating with your hands. Maybe your career in finance has stifled your passion for woodworking. Or you wanted to be a historian but gave up the dream while starting a family or buying an expensive home. Or you had a love for music until your father said you lacked talent. Be open to the possibility that the answers you seek will come soon. You may be surprised where they show up.

If after a week you're still not sure of your direction in life, you probably need to connect more deeply with your inner self, excavating your way through mounds of debris that have built up over the years. To dig deeper, read on.

MINING YOUR PASSION

Clearing the way for a life purpose to emerge is less laborious than it sounds. For best results, you will need three excavating tools: a willingness to feed your needs, an ability to exercise patience and persistence, and the presence to talk to your heart.

Feeding Your Needs

A forward momentum in life emerges as soon as you discover what's holding you back. In most instances, the culprit is at least one hungry need that is closely associated with your self-image. Undernourished, it intrudes on your thinking. It crowds out impulses emanating from your heart, prevents you from feeling good about yourself, and distances you from the aspects of life you value most, such as love, achievement, or freedom. You may already be on your path of purpose but unable to see it because you're not providing for this need.

For example, suppose you love to teach and have needs for attention, independence, and prosperity. Speaking to large audiences, in either live or televised performances, would allow you to best further your purpose. Instead, you've been providing students with one-on-one tutorial services, which leaves you frustrated and discouraged. If the struggle continues to outweigh the rewards, you may eventually abandon your purpose. This dynamic propels many people to leave careers they love.

During my initial session with Jim, an attorney, he said he wanted to dump his law firm and be a high school teacher instead. I asked him to avoid taking action for ninety days while exploring his needs and identifying the intolerable aspects of his law practice. When the ninety days were up, he opted to restructure his career rather than abandon it. During his period of exploration, he had recalled his reasons for becoming an attorney twenty years earlier—to meet his needs for helping others, feeling important, and having a job that challenged him to grow—most of which were currently being satisfied. He also realized he had no burning need for independence and control. In fact, he disliked his position as proprietor, preferring job security and less stress. Two years later, Jim dissolved his firm with no regrets. He now works happily as a county prosecutor.

Hungry needs can weigh anyone down. If you are disgruntled with your job, primary relationships, or living arrangements, see if your unhappiness is due to the conditions of your situation, as opposed to the daily tasks you perform. If it is, chances are that you are on your path of purpose but important needs are not being met. Once you identify these needs and begin to feed them, you will feel more buoyant. The following exercise can help.

FIGURE 4–2

Satisfying Hungry Needs

This is an exercise in three parts. The first part, uncovering dissatisfied aspects of yourself, requires honesty. If you don't own up to a need, it will own you. The second part, prioritizing your needs, calls for discernment. Part three, feeding your hungry needs, calls upon your expertise in practicing the four components of resiliency described in chapter 2: desire, willingness, creativity, and courage.

- Read through this list of needs,* which expands upon those you identified on page 43. Circle the needs that are important to you.

I need:		
Acceptance	Respect	To be liked
Achievement	Praise	To feel honored
Appreciation	To be busy	To be the center of attention
To be desired	To be touched	To be cared about
To be right	To be morally right	To feel understood
Accuracy	To feel helpful	To be in control
To be in the know	Prosperity	Acknowledgment
Challenge	Adventure	Excitement
To win	To possess	To be adored
Honesty	Comfort	Quiet time
To be loved	To be needed	To be important
Safety	Freedom	Independence
Clarity	Order	Consistency
Fun	Balance	Stability
Harmony	To be pain free	To be at peace

- Of the needs you circled, underline the five that most dominate your life right now. (Their intensity indicates that they are not being fulfilled.)

- Do what you can to satisfy these five needs. This task may simply require you to ask others to help you feel more appreciated, or to arrange for more quiet time or more adventure. Or it may require you to radically alter your conditions to give you more control, more chances to be helpful, or more fun.

*Adapted from Coach University's Needless Assessment

Once you understand that your needs are internally driven and that you alone are responsible for feeding them, you can stop expecting others to make you feel good. Hungry needs cause misery and loneliness. Fulfilled needs eradicate the boundaries between "I" and the surrounding world. Absorbed in activity, you are able to see your purpose and align with it. At that point, you enter the vertical world of living in the moment, where you become too busy serving your purpose to bother with worrying, analyzing, and obsessing over what you don't have. You keep dancing after the music stops.

If you are caretaking, apprenticing, or otherwise unable to immediately fulfill your needs, calmly define what it will take to feel respected, honored, and happy with yourself. Then, rather than demand that your needs be met, ask yourself, "What will it take to feel satisfied *until* my needs can be met?" All the while, take care of yourself as best you can. Summon the courage to continue your commitment for a specified period of time. To prevent burnout, frequently remind yourself that you've chosen this path out of a desire to love yourself first.

Isolating, prioritizing, and feeding your needs opens a channel through which your purpose can speak to you. This self-awareness then wakes up your senses to the world around you. Options will appear as you grow and change.

Being Patient and Persistent

Is your passion still eluding you? If so, be patient. Discovering your life's purpose may take time. As Sarah Ban Breathnach says, "We need time to consider, time to reflect, time to make creative choices, time to emerge from the cocoon, time to clean out our closets, and time to clear away psychic cobwebs so that we might pare down to our essence." For now, declare your search for meaning as your present purpose. Knowing you're on the pathway to your heart can be joyous and fulfilling. Have faith that your purpose will emerge. With faith, you can relax and hear important clues. There's no need to race off in search of purpose.

Just as pain, struggle, and loss convey valuable lessons, so does patient optimism. Every day affords a new opportunity to greet your calling. As each day dawns, delight in exploring your talents, liberating your creativity, and trying something new. Take a plunge into unknown territory. You have nothing to lose but boredom.

Persist also in surrounding yourself with people who encourage your excavations. Changing who you are is apt to leave you highly vulnerable to others' opinions of you. With this in mind, declare yourself independent of people who respond to you with doubt and criticism. Invest in relationships that support your development. Release those that keep you small.

Say "no" as well as "yes," not only to people but to activities, thoughts, and emotions. Say "no" to anything that blocks you, internally or externally. Say "yes" to whatever will help you clear a channel to your heart.

Talking to Your Heart

The heart is more aligned with universal flow than the head is. Actors, inventors, successful entrepreneurs, and social leaders alike describe how, at the moment they made the decision to face their fears and go after their dreams, Providence stepped in. Coincidences unfolded. Roadblocks gave way to lucky breaks. You, too, can learn to listen to your heart and follow its dictates. Then trust that what turns up will be right for who you are at that moment. As my mother used to say, "Don't worry, dear. Things always turn out for the best."

How do you know you're on the right track? Ask your heart if your purpose is close at hand. Then, after discovering your purpose, periodically ask your heart if your purpose remains the same or if it is time for something new. Check to see if at any point you are opting for security over passion. When you wake up in the morning, talk to your heart. In the dentist's waiting room, talk to your heart. While driving home in traffic, talk to your heart.

Never stop asking your heart if you are living your purpose. Even if you flip a coin to let heads and tails make the decision for you, your heart will respond. It will send you a message of relief and happiness, or of restlessness and disappointment. Pay attention to its wisdom.

The value of relying on this open channel of communication is revealed in the following parable about a hunter and a parrot.

A hunter from India, famous for trapping exotic and rare species of birds, traveled far and wide. On one of his journeys, he came upon a cave of beautiful parrots with multicolored wings and long, iridescent tails. Silently, he entered the cave. From his corner near the entrance, he could hear the parrots speaking to one another in a language he understood.

At nightfall, when the parrots were asleep, the hunter captured one and took it home for a pet, locking up his prize in a cage. At first, the parrot was heartbroken. It would not eat or speak. The hunter bought only the best food and spent hours reading stories and singing to his bird. Eventually, the bird ate the food, began to speak, and grew to love the hunter.

Two years later, the hunter announced that he was returning to the region where the parrot used to live. The parrot asked the hunter to go to the cave and inform its friends that it was okay. It was happy in its new home, was well cared for, and had no problems.

The hunter, despite much difficulty, found the cave. Startled, the birds listened to his message. When the hunter finished speaking, one of them stiffened and fell to the cave floor, dead.

Upon his return home, the hunter reluctantly told his parrot about the death of its friend. At the word *dead*, the parrot's eyes rolled into its head, its body stiffened, and it keeled over. The hunter shrieked. Scooping up his bird, he carried it outside and, remorseful that he had shocked it to death, prayed for forgiveness. He then set the bird on a grassy knoll in the shade of an old tree. As the hunter wept, the bird suddenly flew to the top limb of the tree. The hunter jumped up and exclaimed, "You tricked me!"

"I'm sorry I had to trick you," the parrot replied. "My friend in the cave was sending me a message through you. He wanted me to know that if I was living contentedly in a cage, I might as well be dead. He was right. I had lost my freedom and, removed from family and friends, my sense of purpose. My passion for living had left me." With that, he circled the hunter's head three times and soared off in a glorious blaze of color.

Now is the time to take flight. Don't wait until there's enough money, the kids are grown, or you find another job. Whenever you hear yourself say, "I would, but...," see the "but" as a lock on the door of your cage. Self-examination takes guts. Yet it will free you to be yourself—alive and free.

Victor Frankl proposes that the search for meaning awakens the spirit. Seeking, on its own, releases your spirit and awakens you to the moment.

Gather your courage. Step onto your path. Feel the fire grow. Whether you are aware of your purpose or searching for it, welcome each new day with a passion for life.

CHAPTER 5

Visioning and Covisioning

When we see clearly from our hearts . . .
we can see hope inside of despair,
direction in the midst of chaos,
and options inside challenges.

—Pat Sullivan

The slogan reads, "Even flights of imagination need a place to soar," heralding American Airlines' commitment to support community arts. But the words hold a deeper meaning. They suggest that ideas need dreams in which to roost so that they can gain visibility. Too many people with intelligence, talent, and creativity lose their drive when they cannot see how to channel their passion.

A purpose, then, is not enough. It needs to find its way into the world through a clear vision. As early-twentieth-century political and social activist Emma Goldman said, "When we can't dream any longer, we die."

The most enduring approach is to portray our purpose in an observable format. Whether we render it in words, hand-drawn images, or pictures cut out and pasted on poster board, crystallizing our desires can generate the resources and energy needed to spring them to life.

Last January, after moping through the holidays and spending the next week too sick with the flu to leave home, I developed a serious case of the "poor me's." To top it off, three contracts fell through and four clients terminated their coaching. One afternoon, frustrated with the muck of self-pity I was wallowing in, I made a cup of tea and retreated to my sacred place. After lighting candles and incense, and turning on soft music, I gazed at the picture of my vision—a collage of what I want to create during the year—that hangs on the wall. That night I felt much calmer as I fell asleep.

The next morning, noticing a lingering thread of fear in the pit of my stomach, I took a brisk walk. As I stepped along, gratitude welled up within me because I had recuperated enough to be outdoors and in motion. Before long, I was acknowledging the many opportunities ahead of me. I even saw beauty in the down time I'd had, for it gave me a chance to remember my purpose, renew my vision, and humbly bring my "being" into the forefront of my awareness. Upon returning from my walk, I sat down to write. If my heart could smile, I'd describe its expression as a satisfied grin.

Even in healthy times I need spiritual Drano. I can go for days fueled with energy, moving passionately in the moment. Then I clog up. To clear out, I gaze at the picture of my vision and, if necessary, step outside for an invigorating walk. On this ocean we call life, my vision is my lifeboat. I ride in it when the current is steady. I cling to it after falling into rough waters. Supported by my vision while writing, coaching, speaking, or sitting quietly, I maintain a sense of harmony with the ebb and flow of life. Like the Greek hero Ulysses, I tie myself to the mast to avoid being lured by distractions and smashing into rocks. Always, my vision is waiting for me, reminding me of who I am and what I'm doing.

People who lack vision struggle repeatedly, treading water with all their might to keep their heads dry. Eventually they exhaust themselves. In fact, psychologist Sydney S. Jourard has found that many American men die from heart disease soon after they retire. Lacking a purposeful future, they slip into a passionless life, at which point their health begins to fail.

A future you can vision clearly in your mind, or covision with another person, gives your purpose a dwelling place. Without it, your passion may sputter out, leaving you to plod endlessly through the horizontal world. With it, your passion can be energized, both fueling your willingness to act and elevating your set-point of happiness.

VISIONING

A vision is something we can see. It's a three-dimensional picture of our desires—a virtual-reality program of our own design. Our visions portray us at our best while accomplishing our purpose one day in the future.

Visions essentially provide destinations, or points of arrival, that direct our energy and decision making. Rather than end points, they are pieces of a bigger puzzle we put together to understand the meaning of our lives. As such, you may not be able to see your purpose beyond the next few years, which is fine. Your current vision will give you guidance until another one replaces it.

Rules for Visioning

There are two rules for portraying a vision. The first is to define it in concrete visual terms, replete with nouns and verbs. Adjectives, such as the word *good* in "I want to be a good parent" and *successful* in "I want to be a successful manager," describe nothing. Instead, identify the specific traits and behaviors that make a parent good and a manager successful.

The second rule is that a vision must extend beyond today's reality. Its function is to help you stretch outside of your comfort zone and move past any fears that have previously stopped you. *Possibility* is the key word. Life coach and author Laura Berman Fortgang says to think a big game when you vision. "If you wish for the stars and only get the moon," she notes, "you've still achieved more than those still stuck in one place on earth."

In going beyond today's reality, however, avoid fantasies whose attainment would take either winning the lottery or divine intervention. For example, reject physical desires that would require a miracle, such as adding inches to your height. And don't vision yourself jet-setting around the world if your savings account is empty. Shoot for the stars. And make sure you have a vehicle that will take you there.

With your purpose at hand and your description of it concretely defined and geared to the future, you're well on your way to rendering an image of your desires. See if it's clear enough to propel you beyond your present circumstances by practicing this exercise.

FIGURE 5–1

Testing the Clarity of Your Vision

To determine whether or not you have consolidated your desires into a lucid vision, follow these instructions.

- Communicate your aspirations to another person.

- Ask this person to rephrase your statements, describing your desires in their own words.

- If the two pictures match, you've achieved sufficient clarity and can begin to portray your vision (see pages 109–115). If the pictures don't match, you have more clarifying to do.

Clarifying Your Vision

It could be that you have no clue what you want tomorrow to look like. If so, write your life purpose on a sheet of paper. Then, using the Life Areas Assessment (figure 5–2), determine the areas of your life that presently support you in achieving your purpose and those that do not. For example, if you want to be a community leader, are you maintaining your physical and emotional health, and taking care of your family? Do your finances give you sufficient freedom to immerse yourself in community affairs?

Next, consider the areas in your life that are governed by "shoulds" rather than "coulds." Are there any "shoulds" in your relationships or career that are keeping you from pursuing your purpose? For instance, do you feel obligated to spend time with friends who bring you down? Are you forgetting to take care of yourself because your family constantly needs you to take care of them? Are you expected to work a twelve-hour day, thereby eliminating time for exercise and intimacy? Whenever you say, "I should be doing...," be careful. "Should be's" are killer bees that can sting the joy right out of you.

Still working with the Life Areas Assessment, envision who you are in each facet of your life. Are you who you think you should be, based on your education and social status, or who your parents or friends want you to be? Or are you a true expression of your passion and joy? Look inside for this picture. As the eminent Swiss psychologist Carl Jung has said, "Your vision will become clear only when you can look into your own heart. Who looks outside, only dreams. Who looks inside, awakes."

Once you have identified life areas that are out of alignment with your purpose or shadowed by "shoulds," ask yourself if you will commit to changing these pictures. Altering them calls for an investment of time and energy, not the addition of yet another obligation. Of course, there may be areas you are not yet ready to modify. For now, focus on those you *are* willing to change. Decide how you can enhance them to better align with your purpose. In making the shift, you won't just be creating a new relationship, job, or home environment. You'll be transforming your life.

FIGURE 5–2

Life Areas Assessment

Fill in each blank with a "yes" or "no" answer.

	Is this life area in line with my purpose?	Am I doing this my way or someone else's?	Can I visualize a better picture?	Am I ready to commit time and energy to transforming?
Physical Health				
Exercise				
Diet				
Use of time				
Emotional Health				
Self-worth				

	Is this life area in line with my purpose?	Am I doing this my way or someone else's?	Can I visualize a better picture?	Am I ready to commit time and energy to transforming?
Optimism				
Relaxation				
Self-reflection				
Spiritual orientation				
Relationships				
Partner				
Parents				
Children				
Siblings				
Friends				
Coworkers				
Manager				
Customers				
Work/Career				
Job tasks				
Communication				
Atmosphere				
Location				
Resources				
Living Space				
Atmosphere				
Aesthetics				
Location				
Learning				
Career growth				
Personal growth				
Finances				
Expenses				
Savings				
Leisure Time				
Hobbies/Sports				
Vacations				
Volunteering				

Portraying Your Vision

Once you can see your vision—the image of you living fully while moving toward your purpose—prepare to record it. Begin by *selecting a date in the future*. Anchoring your vision to a point in time will inject reality into your dreaming. Yet don't obsess over the date. You are not defining an absolute moment in which everything must come together; you're simply establishing a goal to aim for. I like to vision one year in advance. I do it every New Year's Day to create a clear perspective for the coming year. I also formulate a five-year vision, which seems to change after about three years, to keep a bigger picture in view.

Once you've chosen a date, daydream. Imagine what would make your chosen day perfect. If it is a weekday, include your time at home. After all, how you spend your personal time influences your effectiveness on the job, and vice versa. No matter how much you may try to separate work from play, each draws from or adds to the energy available for the other. When I left my corporate job to start my own business, I visioned what my week would look like when the business was one year old. I set aside two days to coach one-on-one, two days to train and speak, and a buffer day for administrative and marketing tasks. Weekends were for free time only. Each day, I exercised, rested, and spent time with family and friends. It took about two years to settle into this schedule, and I'm still living my vision, although certain elements of it vary from time to time.

While daydreaming, see yourself in action. Observe yourself doing what you currently enjoy, as well as what you'd be doing in life areas that could bring you greater satisfaction. In other words, with photographic clarity, picture yourself engaging in behavior that *fulfills your purpose*. Notice how you feel while going about your daily tasks. How are you talking to yourself and treating yourself? Observe details, such as the food you are eating, the people you are living or working with, the clothes you are wearing, and the car you are driving. As you do, awaken all your senses. In addition to feeling your emotions and seeing yourself in action, touch, hear, smell, and taste the future you want to create.

While visioning, if you have difficulty sensing your ideal circumstances, "reverse" the ones you don't like. For example, if your boss acts like a control freak, imagine him trusting you, respecting your talents, and giving you complete control of a project. Or if your mornings are too rushed, picture yourself showering and dressing at a leisurely pace, drinking a fruit-and-protein smoothie for breakfast, and listening to classical radio on your way to work. Or maybe hear your kids helping with the Saturday chores, leaving you time for a quiet bath or a golf game. Don't get hung up on how to make your vision happen. Simply let your dreams flow. Stick to the *who, what,* and *where.* The *how* will show up in its own time.

When gymnast Mary Lou Rhetton visioned her victory before the 1988 Olympics, she saw herself completing a perfect floor performance, the crowd giving her a standing ovation, the ecstasy she felt at that moment, and her picture on the front of a Wheaties box. The same goes for you. Clearly see yourself captivating your audience as you stand in front of the boardroom, then hear the applause and touch the bonus you earn as a result. Feel the love pouring into your words as you write the book you've longed to birth. Walk with pride through the house you've wanted to build. Laugh with your children at Disneyland. Fantasizing is, according to CEO and best-selling business book author Harvey Mackay, "the most powerful means of achieving a goal." So give yourself permission to daydream in 3-dimensional Technicolor.

Below are guidelines for translating the picture of your life areas at their best into a narrative, an image, and a collage. Whichever medium you choose, let your creativity flow. Remember, you aren't compiling a shopping list; you're shaping your life.

Write what you see. To record your vision in narrative form, you'll need a pencil and a stack of blank paper. You can write your vision anywhere, although for best results choose a spot where you will be comfortable, inspired, and free of interruptions—perhaps in a special room or under a favorite tree.

Once you've settled in, describe on the paper everything you see in the picture of you living your purpose. Reinvent yourself as a person immersed in the abundant pleasures of life. Heed the words of Indian nationalist leader Mahatma Gandhi: "My life is my message." While writing, record the vision of your day as your living message.

Following are two visions rendered in words. The first was written by forty-two-year-old Rose Marie, a recently divorced employee relations specialist. The day she chose to describe was six months in the future.

My Vision

I wake up very early in the morning and am truly happy. I start the day with a strong cup of tea (now that I've broken the coffee habit), and briefly scan the newspaper (instead of reading it front to back). Since it's a beautiful day, I take a walk instead of exercising in the living room. After returning, I shower leisurely and get ready for work, choosing a flattering outfit since I'm at my ideal weight of 135. Because it's Friday, I ride my bicycle to work.

Arriving at the office, I'm eager to begin the challenge of diving into my new project now that I've been named project manager. We're defining a series of educational programs for employees, and other benefits-related programs. I draw up a preliminary draft of the project flow to present as a brainstorming starter to my team. I have lunch with a friend I haven't seen in a while, listening to her tell me about her life, and giving advice only when asked.

I spend the afternoon fine-tuning my goals for the year, in preparation for a meeting with my boss. At this meeting, we will plan my career ladder. As the workday draws to a close, I'm shocked to discover it's over.

I attend a board of directors dinner meeting for the women's not-for-profit organization I've joined. I return home in time to unwind by talking on the phone with a good friend, reading a chapter in an engrossing novel, and reflecting on my day in the pages of my journal.

Rose Marie prepared intensely before committing her vision to paper. Referring to her needs list, she identified the needs that were important to her, including the hungry ones that needed feeding. She then focused on improvements she wanted to make in the life areas of diet and exercise, emotional health, communication with her boss and friends, career development, and volunteering. To feed her needs to help others and to increase the possibility of meeting people, she decided to join the board of a not-for-profit organization. To satisfy her need for balance, she included slowing down in the morning, reading for pleasure in the evening, and writing in a journal. Taking on a new project will increase her job satisfaction, and spending time talking to friends will help her feel that people care about her, filling the void left by her divorce. She wasn't ready to vision a new relationship; she wanted to focus on self-development first.

After writing her vision, Rose Marie read it every day. "When I read my vision out loud," she told me, "I can feel the door to my heart spring open."

The vision below was written by Dick, a salesman and frustrated screenwriter who wanted to expand his love for writing into a full-time career. He saw his ideal day occurring three years in the future.

FIGURE 5–4

My Perfect Day

At 6:00 A.M., I wake up and spring out of bed feeling rested, rejuvenated, and alive with anticipation of what the day will bring. I put on my sweat clothes quietly, so as not to wake my sleeping wife, Rahla, and exit for a half-hour exercise session (aerobics three times a week, weights three times a week). After exercising, I return to our beautiful new home for a shower. Invigorated and refreshed, I eat the delicious breakfast Rahla has prepared and discuss plans for the coming day with her and my son, Chase. I then take Chase to school.

It's now 9:00 A.M. I arrive at my office brimming with ideas. I can't wait to sit down. I scribble some notes about future plot points in the screenplay I'm working on, then begin to plow through the scenes. I am "in the flow."

Before I know it, it's noon and time for a lunch appointment with my lawyer. I arrive at the restaurant with minutes to spare. I choose a healthy, tasty vegetarian dish. We go over the sale of my next script. The lunch is both enjoyable and productive. According to the terms of the sale, I earn a six-figure advance plus a healthy percentage from merchandising and ancillary markets.

Back at my office, I meditate for half an hour. Then I dive into the final scenes of my more recent screenplay, soon completing the first draft of it. I put that project away for a few days to let it "cook" while I gain some perspective on improvements.

I return several calls, including one to my investment counselor. He explains that my financial picture is on track and that I've never been in better financial shape. I feel confident, and grateful to have put my fiscal security back together so quickly and so well. I pause for a moment to thank God for blessing me in this way.

On my drive home, I notice the glorious sunset. I'm grateful to the Creator for providing me with a view to enjoy, eyes to see it with, abundant creativity, and financial rewards that allow me to work at what I love.

Rahla and I prepare dinner while Chase plays with the neighborhood kids. We discuss strategies to enhance her business. We nibble at the salad and each other's ears. Chase comes storming in filled with excitement about his day at school. He tells me all about his science experiment. Once he can sit, we join him at the dinner table, say a prayer of thanks, and eat. Rahla and I marvel at Chase's ideas and self-confidence as he talks about his views of the world. I'm so proud, I could cry.

After dinner, Chase does his homework, I read the mail and newspaper, and Rahla prepares a keynote speech she's planning to give at a conference. Beautiful music fills our house as we work.

Later, I help Chase get ready for bed. I read him a story, and we talk about a recent playground incident. We then play a Beatles CD and sing a song together.

Rahla comes in to say good night and I retire to our room. I light several candles, adding a romantic glow to our little "hideaway." I also light some incense and put on sensuous music. When Rahla joins me, we talk about how wonderfully things are working out. We share a laugh over Chase's antics and we kiss. We make long, slow, passionate love, then fall asleep in each other's arms. A perfect day has come to a perfect conclusion.

Illustrate what you see. A second option is to illustrate your vision by sketching or painting your desires. Begin by touring art, hobby, stationery, or drug stores. Look for glitter, sequins, ribbons, and small party favors to add texture to your composition. Then choose your medium—paint, chalk, crayons, pencils, charcoal, or all of these—and a suitable surface, such as a canvas or poster board.

With your materials set in front of you, close your eyes and visualize yourself living your perfect day. Dance in your ideal house, excel in your ideal career, luxuriate in your ideal romance. Fill in the juicy details. Smell, touch, and taste the pleasures.

Once you are thoroughly aroused, open your eyes and create freely. Perhaps paint a grand scene with broad strokes and splashes of color. Or draw a melange of activities that blend into one. Portray the outcomes you want to bring to life, or depict them symbolically in a flowing river, a sunrise, mountain peaks, and soaring birds. Think magic. Think power and fun. Then reach for a glue stick and sprinkle on sequins. Attach charms, foil strips, and other trimmings. Tape on personal items or draw in personal features to claim the dream as your own.

Kat, a workshop participant, portrayed her vision via watercolors, ribbon, and glitter. Rather than follow a formula, she simply let images dance from her fingers through the paintbrush and onto the canvas. "I felt the energy pour through my fingertips," she explained. "It came alive. And I ended up with a composite of my dreams—not as my mind sees them, but as my soul does."

Create a collage. To construct a collage of your vision, choose magazine pictures and headlines that represent everything you desire for yourself, then paste them on poster board. The result, as always, should inspire positive actions and focus your energy on what you want to have, do, and be.

First, gather your materials. You will need a stack of magazines, travel brochures, mail-order catalogs, or family photos; a pair of scissors; a glue stick; and poster board, preferably 20 by 28 inches.

Second, concentrate on your desires. Review your Life Areas Assessment (see pages 107–108), then ask yourself these questions: "What will I commit to improving in this time frame?" "What would make me feel more satisfied than I am right now?" "Which of my dreams remain unfulfilled?" "What activities would help me live in better alignment with my purpose?" "What stirs my passion?"

Third, select pictures and headlines that best answer these questions. Would you like to go to Tahiti? If so, search for an ocean lined with palm trees. How about owning a new home? In this case, find your dream house or a For Sale sign. An image of two people strolling through a park might represent a romance or more time with your partner. A bottle of Dom Perignon could symbolize success at work.

Finally, cut out and arrange the material you've selected, gluing each piece on the poster board. Arrange them in any way you like, perhaps partitioning your board into sections that you can easily identify. I've designated one corner of mine to my career, another to romance, a third to the material rewards I'd like to manifest, and the fourth to my spiritual goals. The center portion of my board represents my number one focus for the year. Each year, something new occupies the center space.

My friend Joanne Schlosser, author of *Bright Ideas for a Better Life*, uses this method to help people create a "treasure map." Every January, she gathers together a group of friends to design their maps for the coming year. Interestingly, an uncanny number of these people have realized the dreams they previously pasted on their boards. Joanne herself glued two pictures of Hawaii on her first treasure map. A week later, she received an invitation to speak at a conference in Honolulu. The next year, she placed Montana on her map. That summer, she was asked to speak to a group meeting in Glacier National Park. Other people she knows have ended up with the jobs and relationships they posted on their maps. Some attribute these outcomes to coincidence; others, to magic. Joanne is convinced they stem from the power inherent in human energy that is focused on realizing a dream.

Whether you write your vision in words, paint a picture of it, or cut out images of it and paste them on a board, display the finished work prominently, in a place where you will see it each day. As you look at it, ask yourself, "Am I committed to making this happen?" In the next breath, answer aloud, "Yes!"

COVISIONING

Visioning has the power to initiate action. Bringing the action to fruition when it involves other people, requires covisioning. This we do by engaging their cooperation. To covision, we negotiate, blend ideas, and form a combined vision.

For example, Dick's narrative, on pages 112–113, contains many opportunities for covisioning. He may decide to discuss, and possibly negotiate, breakfast preparations with his wife, sales and marketing strategies with his attorney, and evening routines with his son. As a result, Dick would end up with a slightly altered "perfect day," but one that nonetheless reflects the aspirations he most values.

Arriving at mutually rewarding decisions takes time. Yet every hour we give it can spare years of turmoil. After all, a partnership, work arrangement, or family relationship based on conflicting dreams causes disappointments, if not seriously hurt feelings. And the more damage a relationship sustains, the longer the wounds take to heal.

To move in the direction of successful covisioning, follow the four steps outlined below. Adapt them, as needed, to situations you are facing. If you're concerned about unproductive arguing, perhaps ask an objective third party to facilitate the process. Even with a defensive spouse or hard-to-please colleague, covisioning can help you cut through differences and arrive at a mutually agreeable blueprint of your future endeavors together.

Step 1: Communicate your personal visions. A statement commonly heard both at home and in the workplace is, "This isn't at all what I expected." A statement rarely heard is, "Let me tell you exactly what's on my mind." To begin cross-pollinating their expectations, partners and teammates need to feel comfortable articulating their personal visions.

After six months of living in his too-small-for-two condominium, my friend Richard and I decided to buy a house together. It was a challenging mission. When I liked the brightness of a house, Richard hated the floor plan. When he liked the layout, I couldn't cope with the neighbors' proximity. One Sunday morning after four and a half months of locking horns, we decided that if we couldn't find an acceptable dwelling by the end of the day, we would postpone the search indefinitely. As happy endings go, our prayers were answered that afternoon by a house with four bedrooms, large closets, and a backyard shielded from prying eyes.

Less than two years later, I started perusing the newspaper's real estate ads for another home. The arrangement of rooms in ours no longer fit my needs, which hardly surprised me. Having moved twenty-seven times in my adult life, I had no sense of a forever-perfect house. In my experience, changing locations was a regular event.

Richard's perspective was different. Every time he caught me reading the ads, he offered to take me to the movies, to the mall, to see my sister—anywhere my heart desired. When I asked him why he seemed intent on distracting me from my quest, he confessed to dreading another move. He couldn't understand why I wasn't happy, since the house had everything we needed. In his experience, moving was a once-a-decade event.

"But I want my own office," I explained. "Besides, the exercise room is too noisy, and I hate the backyard."

"Why didn't you speak up two years ago?" he asked. "It's no small mortgage we're sitting on."

"I don't know" was all I could say. Assuming the perfect house was nonexistent, I had no idea what it might look like. In short, my vision was fuzzy.

Fortunately, Richard and I solved our problem before it eroded our good feelings for each other. After exploring our desires, I moved my office into the living room, he changed his workout schedule, and we planted more trees in the backyard. No sooner was that done than we began to share the pictures we each held about our future together.

How many times have you faced a similar problem? Did you ever plan your career, your child's education, or a getaway with your partner, then lose your focus when another person's desires obliterated your own? Did you ever feel your wishes silenced by a fear of rejection, of being used, or of disappointment? The best preventive measure is to state what you want clearly to others.

Begin by committing your vision to paper and having the other person do the same with theirs. The more details you both include, the better. Don't wait until "the house" is half built to ask for what you desire.

Step 2: Declare your strongest desires. To clarify the most relevant features of your vision, try this activity. Divide a sheet of paper into two columns, labeling one "Terribles" and the other "Must Haves."

Terribles	Must Haves

Under "terribles," list your three most unwanted outcomes of the project or relationship under consideration. An example might be: "We will let problems simmer and explode before discussing them," "We will make spending decisions without consulting each other," and "We will get into routines and squelch all spontaneity." Under "must haves," list your three most desirable outcomes, such as "We will communicate face-to-face at least once a week," "We will each take up to three weeks of vacation a year," and "We will celebrate our collaborative efforts on a regular basis."

The purpose of this exercise is to understand what each of you considers vital to personal happiness. Although these points may be negotiable, they must somehow be met or your relationship will erode. The other portions of your individual visions are less critical and therefore easier to blend.

Once you have completed your "terribles" and "must haves," sit down together in a quiet, comfortable setting and take turns reading aloud your visions and your lists. The reader reads; the listener listens respectfully, without commenting.

Step 3. Construct a covision. Now is the time to sit down with each other and write a few paragraphs that weave together your individual visions. If your visions and lists are harmonious, you're home free and your covision will flow naturally. If you collide on an issue, stop to work out your differences. If possible, go for a win-win creative solution that meets everyone's needs.

For example, Rose Marie's boss did not end up giving her a project to manage during the first year, but he did coach her on developing a budget for a new department. Once she mastered budgeting and a few other skills they jointly identified, she qualified for the position of manager. As for Dick, he and Rahla hired a neighbor's daughter to prepare breakfast, accommodating both his yearnings for a delicious meal and Rahla's desire to sleep in for an hour.

After ironing out your differences, choose a date of completion or a time of celebration. Then ask the following question: "If we were watching a videotape titled *Our Three-Year Anniversary* or *Our Team-Recognition Dinner*, what would we see and hear?" Together, brainstorm the results you would be celebrating and record your acknowledgments on paper. Include such details as your individual visions and "must haves," as well as the tasks you each performed and the emotions you experienced while living your collective dream. Now organize the ideas into a story that incorporates all the elements of your victory speeches. This story is your covision.

Step 4: Make it happen. Rather than stuff your covision in a drawer, keep it handy. If you reread it periodically, you will begin to manifest it in your actions. With these new actions in place, you will soon see that success depends on collaboration, and that blending yields far better results than expecting and demanding ever could. For one thing, blending imbues a relationship with trust, mutuality, and respect. For another, team members who share a common picture of their purpose experience joy as well as gratifying results. As futurist Bob Treadway says, "A team is genius when it works together."

REVIEWING THE PICTURE

Whether you have visioned on your own or covisioned, review the merits of the picture on a regular basis. As you do, ask yourself three questions: "Is this what I want *right now* or is it something I thought I wanted years ago and have since outgrown?" "Do I feel energized by this picture?" "If my vision comes true, will it bring me pleasure?" The last thing you want to do is wake up one morning to find that you have spent a good portion of your life seeking happiness down the wrong road.

For years Jan, my assistant, could not differentiate her desires from her husband's opinions and her peers' priorities, which left her frustrated and unable to make decisions about her future. Jan worked for me part-time, from ten o'clock until three every weekday but Thursday. She devoted early mornings and late afternoons to her children, and reserved Thursdays for friends. Her income was adequate, although her husband's salary covered the bulk of the family's expenses. Still, she took pride in her work and professional development. Although she'd told me many times that her situation was perfect, when she composed her vision she described herself in a full-time position. Together, we set a date to covision this new picture.

The next day, Jan told me she was uncomfortable with her vision, as was her husband. He wanted her to stay at home with their two young children. But she'd suspected that I, as her employer and friend, would like her vision since I actively supported women in their achievements. Questions flooded my mind: Was Jan's vision of a full-time position really hers? Or was it a sign of rebellion against her husband's domination, coupled with her need to feel valued by a society that ranks professional achievement over motherhood?

After sorting out her feelings, Jan admitted to liking her part-time arrangement after all, because it allowed her to realize her professional potential while also being an involved mother. I asked her to rewrite her vision, leaving her hours as they were but expanding her responsibilities to instill more challenge into her work. She came back with a picture that inspired her, at which point we covisioned a mutually satisfying plan. At the end of our meeting, I suggested that she review the vision annually, since her needs might change as the children grew up.

To avoid serving a purpose that is not yours, review your vision constantly to be sure it honors *you*. If you want to deepen your relationships, for instance, carve in more time with family and friends. In addition to logging in daily blocks for phone calls, letters, and e-mail to people who make you smile, allow for personal "breathing" time and moments for giving prayerful thanks for their love and support. In other words, balance each day with doses of "fire" and "water." That way you'll be ignited by your passion yet able to cool down before burning out.

To keep joy emerging and your desires manifesting, fill your heart with your vision. The following exercise, practiced once a day, will help.

FIGURE 5–5

Engage the Seeing Heart

Because the heart sees even when the eyes grow dim with confusion, visions that reside in the heart are likely to appear in everyday life. To draw your vision into your seeing heart, follow these steps.

- Find a quiet moment at the beginning or end of the day to review your vision.

- Standing comfortably, take a deep breath, stretch your arms overhead, and look toward the sky or the ceiling. See your vision, smile broadly, then exhale.

- While breathing in, imagine your vision flowing into your heart. Hold it in your heart as you hold your breath.

- While breathing out, feel your vision settle into your being.

- Silently express your gratitude for a vision that brings such joy, then slowly lower your arms to your sides.

CHAPTER 6

Bridging the Gap

*Upon completing the universe,
God pronounced it "very good,"
not "perfect."*

—Sarah Ban Breathnach

Do you like to watch great speakers command the stage? Are you intrigued by orators who capture the hearts of a television audience or a classroom of students?

Enchanted by these spellbinding orators, we assume they were born with natural magnetism. Swayed by their power to influence us, we think they've always given perfect performances. Neither assumption is true. Scores of dynamic presenters were once terrified mumblers who, through practice, reassurance from others, and self-forgiveness, learned to speak in front of a group. And even the best speakers, while polished, are not flawless. Like all champions, they practice diligently to stay on top of their game. They commit to bridging the gap between who they are and who they can be, then they hang on tight for the ride.

Bridging the gap means transforming your life so that each succeeding day looks more like your vision. Generating what you want for yourself is something you'll most likely have to work at over time. Yet if you are doing what you love and you're "being" your purpose, the work will be fulfilling. In essence, the secret to living in joy is enjoying your practice.

Does practice make perfect? No—practice makes *easier*. The more you "know your stuff," the more poised you become. Your foundation strengthens. Your power surges. In other words, competence breeds confidence. The more adept you become, the more you can get out of your own way. Why? Because practice frees you to communicate from your heart, not your head. You can float on stage, knowing the right words will come. You can dance around the basketball court, knowing you're able to make the shot. You can converse meaningfully with your partner, knowing how to convey your feelings. Committed practice liberates your voice, your style, and your truth.

If your practice yields more pain than pleasure, however, chances are you're not living your true purpose. Headaches are signals. When you have to force yourself to get up in the morning, to smile at people who cross your path, and to log in hours at a project, something is wrong with your picture. Most likely, it is time to correct your course or start over again. If your practice provides little joy and you cannot change what you're doing just yet, then at least change who you're being. The quicker you can be someone who sees future options instead of present-day problems, the sooner you'll find your path.

So where do you start the bridging? Now that you've created this grand picture of your vision, how do you go about making it real? First, you separate the vision into manageable pieces. Then you devise a plan for manifesting them, steering clear of impasses.

VISION = THE SUM OF ITS PARTS

Ideally, a glance at the picture of your vision will pump your heart and launch you into action. But if you don't know where to start, or if you focus on one portion of the picture at the expense of the others, you may stall out or find yourself derailed.

To insure against such catastrophes, separate your vision into four parts—spirit, relationships, rewards, and your life's work, as is illustrated in figure 6–1, on page 126. Then devise a plan that incorporates a balance of activities from each area.

Spirit

Which components of your vision revive your spirit? Do you exercise, cook comfort foods, sing songs, go to your place of worship, or take quiet morning walks? Activities performed with your lover, your children, or in the course of fulfilling your life's work can revive your energy; but for purposes of bridging, identify endeavors that you do alone to uplift your spirit. Rose Marie, described in chapter 5, saw herself tending to her spirit during her morning drive and while writing in her gratitude journal in the evening. Richard identified exercise, prayer, stopping to appreciate the sunset, filling his house with music, and eating nutritious foods as replenishment for his soul. On busy days, I tend to nurture mine by listening to Beethoven's Fifth Symphony and taking work breaks to pet my cat.

What activities do you find soothing or inspiring? List them, including those that you reserve for quiet times, such as meditating, and those that you blend with daily tasks.

Relationships

What portions of your vision enhance your relationships? Cite specific interactions with your family, friends, partner, coworkers and colleagues, neighbors, and even enemies who show up in your vision. Rose Marie imagined a successful interchange with her boss and more involvement in her conversations with friends. Richard visioned both intimate and fun-loving exchanges with his family and business associates.

List the relationships you identified in your vision. Then describe *who* you are while interacting with these people and *how* your encounters unfold. For instance, you may see yourself being patient with your boss as you brainstorm win-win solutions together. Identifying who you are in your relationships and how you want them to unfold helps shape the outcomes that serve your purpose.

Rewards

The vacations, cars, and new houses in your vision are your just desserts. When I walk down the steps in my house, for example, my heart swells at the sight of the beautiful landscape out the windows and of various mementos from my travels. These delights symbolize personal achievement. My home is a spiritual harbor where I can rest between adventures. It's not big. It's not in the classiest part of town. But it does fulfill my desire for beauty and peace. It's a well-deserved reward for staying on track with my purpose.

Name the rewards you've included in your vision. Beside each material item, identify what it represents to you and the personal satisfaction you will derive from it.

Your Life's Work

The fourth area of your vision encompasses everything you do with the intention of achieving your purpose, or what you see as your role on the planet. Everything you formulate, give birth to, develop, extend, sell to others, help others achieve, adapt to, overcome, become, improve, and complete falls within the realm of your life's work. Rose Marie envisioned both her career development and community activities as her life's work. Richard's work was to spread happiness through his writing and to fashion a harmonious home life.

List the elements of your life's work. Include your professional endeavors, your volunteer contributions, your household tasks, your inventions and compositions, the results you manifest with others, and the masterpieces you conceive on your own.

While segmenting your vision into these four parts, you may notice that some activities have a dual function. Those that do should be assigned to the area they most strongly contribute to. For instance, although writing empowers my soul, its primary function is to fulfill my life's work. Whereas playing with your children may soothe your spirit and align you with your life's purpose, its strongest function may be to strengthen your relationship with them; if so, list it under "relationships."

Ultimately, each area needs to work in harmony with the others. Your spirit, relationships, and rewards should enhance the energy you have for your life's work. Likewise, the pursuit of your life's work will bring you the most happiness when you are also nurturing your spirit, relationships, and rewards. The reason for allocating an activity to only one portion of your vision is to sort out the pieces so that with board, hammer, and nail in place, you can assemble this do-it-yourself project called life.

FIGURE 6–1

The Parts of Your Vision

Spirit	Relationships	Rewards	Your Life's Work
What revives and nourishes you?	Who are you with and how do you interact?	What tangible items demonstrate your success to you, and why?	What are you doing, creating, and becoming?

DESIGNING A STRATEGY

Closing the gap between your vision and your present-day reality is much like building a bridge. If the bridge is well designed and sturdily built, you will have no trouble crossing it. Here are some pointers to get you started.

Implementation Plan

Below is a three-step procedure for building a bridge to your vision. While following these steps, refer to your completed lists in figure 6–1.

1. **Rate each item by frequency.**

   Using a scale of values from 1 to 10, rank every item listed in each of the four categories. Assign a value of 1 to items that are virtually nonexistent in your life today, and a value of 10 to those you practice regularly.

   For example, in the spirit category Rose Marie gave her morning routine a 2 since she rarely used the time to her advantage, and her evening ritual a 4 because she spent some evenings each week reading and connecting with friends. Adding weekend items to her list—namely, hiking, attending outdoor concerts, and listening to soft jazz while bathing—she assigned these activities a 7, 5, and 9, respectively.

2. **Choose an activity in each category.**

   In each category, circle one item you'd like to concentrate on immediately. Limit your selections to the activities ranked from 4 to 8.

3. **Integrate the chosen activities into your life.**

   Begin by selecting one of the circled items—preferably the one you most like spending time on. Focus on this activity for the next three weeks. (Remember, it takes about twenty-one days of awareness and practice to change a mental habit.) To enhance your concentration, post reminders around your home, in your car, and at your workplace.

   Once you have integrated this activity into your life, spend three weeks focusing on a circled item in another category. Continue in this manner until you have incorporated all four circled items into your day-to-day existence. After twelve weeks of focused integration on the rotating categories, your life will be greatly enriched.

Repeat this procedure, rerating each item on your list, circling four new mid-range activities, and integrating them into your life. After raising your scores on the mid-range items, you'll find the "hard stuff" easier to achieve.

Troubleshooting

Although your bridge-building is apt to prove highly effective, minor problems may arise. For instance, what if one of your circled items, such as buying a car or traveling around the world, is currently beyond your reach? If an undertaking you've chosen is beyond your means to complete, then either start small—perhaps saving money for the car or researching options for the trip—or set a related goal that is more readily accessible. The following story demonstrates how you can rein in a faraway dream.

After two frustrating years of procrastination, Carol went to Cuernavaca, south of Mexico City, to study Spanish. She attended classes during the day and spent nights visiting with her host family. Lucy, the mother, took special interest in Carol. Their after-dinner conversations lasted until midnight as she probed for details about Carol's life. Although Carol was at first happy to answer her questions, she soon tired of the one-sidedness of their discussions.

On the third evening, Carol refused to talk until Lucy revealed more about herself. Lucy apologized for being nosy. "Ever since I was a little girl, I've wanted to travel the world," she explained. "But I am poor, and I now have a family to care for."

"You still can," Carol said. "When your kids grow older—"

Lucy closed her eyes and shook her head. "It's okay," she explained. "I've found a better way. Instead of running off to see the world, I bring it to me."

She handed Carol a stack of photographs showing men and women of various cultures and ages posed in front of her house. "I've seen so much of the world—England, Israel, Australia," she said. "And people pay me for my travels. Do you know anyone else with such a fine arrangement?"

The next morning, Lucy took a picture of Carol standing in front of her house. Carol, in turn, used the automatic setting on her camera to photograph the two of them together. She planned to frame the portrait and hang it as a visible reminder to remain flexible while designing her life rather than rigidly affixed to a difficult goal.

If you, like Carol, are always looking ahead, you may miss the bridging possibilities that exist under your nose. Don't compromise your dreams, of course. But do recognize the many vehicles that can take you there. In the words of George Bernard Shaw, "The people who get on in this world are those who get up and look for the circumstances they want, and if they can't find them, they make them."

No matter how far away it may seem, every dream has a starting point. But if you convince yourself that you need more time, money, or skills in order to move forward, you may never get there. To guard against a future darkened by regrets of "I wish I would have . . ." or "I could have been more . . . ," plan this year's and next year's calendar now. Reserve time for fun vacations and weekends. Mark the days you will go to the gym, sign up for that weekly massage, start your own business, take dance lessons, join a discussion group, or research the best cruises for singles. Highlight anniversaries and birthdays to celebrate. Block out days for reflection and contemplation. Take the Nike corporation's advice and "Just do it."

Out-of-reach goals are one potential problem in bridge-building. Another is the temptation to tackle several circled items at once. For instance, you may decide to allocate three weeks to cultivating both your spirit priority and your relationship priority, since they appear easy to accomplish. This practice is not recommended. Dispersed energy will slow you down considerably. A single focus produces visible results much more quickly. After all, while building the bridge between your present reality and your vision, you can lay only one board at a time. So stick with one item on your list until it is part of your life, *then* move on to the next.

Bridging the gap is a process of becoming, not acquiring. You'll be growing, digressing, leaping, wandering, and learning for the rest of your life. You might as well enjoy the scenery.

GROUND RULES FOR CROSSING THE BRIDGE
The following ground rules will help you approach your vision with the least amount of struggle. You'll feel lighter and more wakeful. Better yet, you'll gain a surer sense of your life's purpose.

Rule #1: Take pleasure in patience and persistence.
Living happily ever after starts today, with a commitment to your vision and a disciplined approach to its attainment. Discipline, in this context, means the act of caring for life's gifts. No matter which part

of your vision you are focusing on—whether you're tending to yourself, your family, your job, or your car—regular acts of refining, repairing, renewing, improving, and celebrating show gratitude for the gifts you've been entrusted with. Moving consistently toward improved ratings in your four vision areas is both a tribute to yourself and a thank-you note to God.

Commitment requires patience and persistence, all the more so in times of error or oversight. Mistakes happen. Yet fumbles need not be labeled "failures." Actress Mary Pickford said, "This thing we call 'failure' is not the falling down, but the staying down"—in short, the giving up. People who have a passion to succeed fall down, stand back up, and keep going, all the while learning from their miscalculations. Basketball legend Michael Jordon gave a new twist to failure when he said: "I have missed more than nine thousand shots in my career. I have lost almost three hundred games. On twenty-six occasions I have been entrusted to take the game-winning shot . . . and missed. And I have failed over and over and over again in my life. And that is why I succeed."

Patience and persistence propel us toward success in every arena of life. Take pleasure in them and you will reap bountiful rewards—personal fulfillment, joyful relationships, and delightful work experiences. Even leisurely activities, such as playing tennis, meditating, watching the sunset, or learning the nuances of fine wines, begin to "hum" when approached with patient persistence.

For now, stubbornly persist. The day will come when you no longer think about it. The commitment to growth will be a part of who you are.

If you find no joy in your pursuit, however, reconsider this portion of your vision. Your unhappiness could be a signal to modify the item you are striving to attain, or to alter your vision. Remember, your ultimate commitment is not to numbly endure, but to powerfully transform.

Rule #2: Quit chasing the fantasy of perfection.

Perfection kills joy. Perfection convinces you that if you don't hit the mark you're defective. If you don't look like the model on this week's glitziest magazine cover, you're doomed. If you lose your job, your love, or your car keys, you're worthless. Chasing the illusion of perfection breeds frustration, discouragement, and anger. The pressure never lets up. Even if one day you are graced with a fabulous body, place of employment, mate, or golf swing, the ecstasy will quickly fade to despair as you find new flaws to obsess about.

Here's the rub: *You're perfect just the way you are.* If you accept what you have in the present moment, you can clearly see what you must do to achieve the results you want. The question is not, "Why are others better than me?" but rather, "How can I do my best with the gifts I have?" All forward motion hinges on recognizing your accomplishments, not your faults. Strive to do your best. Then acknowledge that your best is perfect.

"The gem cannot be polished without friction, nor man perfected without trials," Confucius said. So give yourself permission to be wrong, flawed, and incomplete, and the courage to explore new vistas without self-judgment. Instead of worrying about perfection, heed the words of writer and magazine editor Wendy Reid Crisp, who tells us, "Anything that is worth doing is worth doing half-assed."

Imagine sitting at the breakfast table beside a window, enjoying the morning air. The warmth of the sun feels so good that you open the kitchen door to freshen up the room. No sooner do you sit back down than a fly buzzes in, hitting the far wall, then heading for the window. *Bam!*—it hits the pane. Desperate to reach its goal, it buzzes repeatedly, struggling to ram itself through the glass. Finally it falls, exhausted, to the window ledge. You scoop up the fly with your newspaper and set it outside on the porch. Moments later, it lifts off and soars away.

While chasing the fantasy of perfection you, like the fly, work yourself to exhaustion, perhaps coupled with humiliation, trying to make yourself into something you are not. However, when you stop beating yourself up with judgment and scorn, you wake up knowing that you are on the perfect path for you and ready to take the next step.

Be persistent, yet also present. Joy is in the moment, not the future or the past. Look around you. The sun rises. Birds sing. The morning coffee smells great. Steam from the mug warms your nose. Jelly spreads smoothly on the toast. Taste buds work. All is right with the world, and you are "being" in the perfect place and time. Remind yourself of your purpose. Fire up your passion. Then live the rest of the day in your power. Bridging is not about sticking to deadlines and reaching rigid goals. It's about living your life on a steady and fulfilling path.

Rule #3: Stop comparing yourself with others.

Why waste time and energy with "better than" and "less than" self-evaluations? Assess your progress regularly, but when you do, compare yourself only with *yourself*. Remember, wherever you are now is perfect because that's all there is. Each present moment is your benchmark from which to evaluate your growth.

The next time you catch yourself feeling envious, smug, or small, recognize that you are rating yourself against someone on a different mission. This person has their own lessons to learn. Each of us walks a unique path in life.

Instead of slipping into comparisons, commend yourself for each step you have taken toward your vision, concentrating on your own efforts and achievements. If you admire some aspect about the other person, ask them to help you. They will feel good and you, having swallowed your pride enough to reach out, will have grown.

There is no growth, however, in proving to others what you know. Attempting to prove ourselves to anyone is a waste of time and shuts down our channels to learning. In response, our skills and knowledge, like unexercised muscles, atrophy. As public speaker Danielle Kennedy says, "Are you green and growing, or are you ripe and rotten?"

Proving ourselves to others is also a setup for failure. When we push for attention and validation, we rarely get enough to meet our needs. Then sooner or later our passion smolders and the embers give rise to compulsions. The horizontal world of doing becomes all-consuming, its triumphs granting only momentary rewards.

If you are addicted to proving yourself and yearn to be free of it, reprogram your subconscious. The six-step program outlined below can hasten your recovery.

Figure 6–2

Six Steps to Freedom from "Proving"

The compulsion to prove ourselves to others is rooted in insecurity and a deep-seated need for approval from others. In moving toward self-approval, you free yourself to stretch and grow. Self-

---

approval increases each time you change an undesirable behavior or mental habit, which the following steps can help you accomplish.

1. Imagine thinking, feeling, and behaving as if it doesn't matter how others have judged you. See yourself going about your day caring for yourself more than worrying about the approval of others.

2. Describe the day in a few paragraphs, noting each detail as if you were recounting it to another person.

3. Read the description to a friend. Ask them to inquire about your progress at least once a week for the next month.

4. Read the description to yourself every morning and evening for 21 days. Any time you slip into "proving" behaviors, shift your focus to *creating*. Let go of the need for approval. Come to peace with yourself through creativity.

5. At the end of each day, acknowledge the progress you made. Then once a week celebrate your growth, no matter how minuscule it may be. Buy a new CD; toast yourself with a glass of champagne or sparkling cider; take a long, soothing bath.

6. After 21 days, ask yourself if the new habit has taken hold. If it hasn't, repeat this program. If it has, congratulate yourself for loving who you are.

Rule #4: Keep your mind open.
When people give you advice or information, detach from your judgment. Don't just stop your mind from judging. Instead, catch yourself criticizing their statements, perhaps muttering to yourself, "That's stupid—I don't agree." Then remove these critical thoughts from your head, clearing space for new thoughts to come in. Let the advice float around your brain for a while. Later, when you have time to yourself, take a closer look at the suggestions. Consider the outcomes that might arise if you were to act on the proffered ideas. Accept the information

that's potentially useful to you and dump the rest. Always see your mind as a cup half full, with plenty of room for receiving.

Advice and information, like diamonds in the rough, often strike us as useless lumps of dirt. Instead, think of them as raw materials that must be cleaned up and analyzed before they can shine. Keep your mind open to learning from other people's experiences and you may find a surprising number of gems worth keeping.

Business writer Lisa Goff says, "People who lead have to be open to new ideas. The extent to which a company can encourage new ideas is the extent to which its competitive edge is sustainable." The same is true of life. The extent to which you take in points of view different from your own, the faster you'll grow, and the more you'll feel like an integral member of the human collective.

Rule #5: Go at your own pace.
Change calls for stretching. Yet stretching can be uncomfortable—so much so that you may not want to do it again. If that's your decision, don't stop crossing the bridge; just slow down. Move toward your vision at a pace you feel ready for.

Continually set realistic expectations for yourself. If you don't act on an intention today, take to heart the words of Scarlett O'Hara: "Tomorrow is another day." It takes time to breathe life into dreams.

Any time you face a challenge that robs you of pleasure, determine whether the culprit is in your head, your body, or your life circumstances. Then decide which facets are in your power to change and which are out of your present reach. Ask yourself, "How can I feel comfortable enough to take the next step toward my vision?" Then either prepare a new plan and timeline that will enable you to proceed with confidence, or open yourself to seeing a prettier path.

Even though bridging the gap between your present reality and your vision requires you to "do" things, be mindful of "who you be." Draw pleasure from persevering, see perfection in the present moment, love yourself just as you are, clear your mind to accept new ideas, then take all the time you need. No one is chasing you. Bridging the gap is about pursuing your dreams. Tend to your growth, not your goals. Using your heart as well as your head, you will find what you most want for yourself.

CHAPTER 7

The Possibility Game

*Trust that it went the way
it was supposed to go—
and it always turns out to be better.*

—Lee Glickstein

I magine that you and your partner planned a weekend getaway on the northern California coast beginning next Saturday. The cabin you rented sits on a forested hill overlooking the ocean. You've just completed a big project, working ten- to twelve-hour days for two months, and sacrificing most of your weekends to catch up on chores you neglected during the week. You can't wait to board the airplane. Unencumbered by your computer and cell phone, you're determined to enjoy this vacation.

You leave work early Friday. Once home, you notice the message indicator on the telephone is flashing, but you ignore it, opting to start your vacation now. While packing, you picture you and your partner wandering through the dense redwood forest. As the day starts to warm, you come upon a stream with rocks large enough to sunbathe on. Then you retreat to the cabin, in the shade of a huge stand of old trees. That evening, you dine at a romantic restaurant in the town nearby. Dessert is back at the cabin—sipping champagne in the hot tub on the deck. Luxuriating in bed hours later, you are lulled to sleep by the sounds of rhythmic ocean waves, grateful for a weekend in paradise.

When you head for the kitchen to pack your vitamins, the flashing light on the phone again catches your eye. Your daydream fades as you give in and hit the button. The message is from the owner of the cabin. "So sorry to tell you this, but you shouldn't plan on arriving tomorrow. We've had two full days of a heavy downpour. The roads are flooded and the highway department, concerned about landslides, has posted an advisory warning. The Weather Bureau is predicting heavy rains throughout the weekend. We're hoping the cabin will be okay, but we can't be sure, and we certainly can't risk having you stay there. Sorry. Please call to reschedule your reservation."

How do you react? Basically, you have three choices. *Choice number one:* Scream, rant, and curse life for being so cruel. Dump your suitcase on the floor. Spend the weekend complaining, and griping endlessly about your partner's annoying habits. *Choice number two:* Curse the cabin owner while driving back to the office. Decide to spend the weekend catching up on paperwork. *Choice number three:* Exhale . . . then sit down and plan an enjoyable weekend at home with your partner. Read a good novel. Nibble on popcorn at a double feature. Take a long bath together. Get a massage. Gaze at the midnight sky. Explore the nooks and crannies of your hometown, seeking out interesting shops and restaurants.

So what's your decision? The Talmud says that when we die, we're held accountable for every moment of pleasure we've passed up. The Koran declares joy a human responsibility. The Buddha said wisdom comes from delighting in the ordinary. Finding a hint of happiness honors the presence of God. Choosing to cruise—to go with the flow and make circumstances enjoyable—is a way of saying thank you for being alive.

We live in a sea of possibilities. Although we are dealt circumstances, conditions, and events, how we respond to them is up to us. In fact, choice-making is our "response-ability." In the words of author Dorothy Gilman, "It's when we're given choice that we sit with the gods and design ourselves." Each time you sit with the gods in this way, you are playing the possibility game.

Psychology professor Mihaly Csikszentmihalyi says it is useful to regard attention—the thinking, remembering, feeling, and analyzing going on at any given moment in your brain—as "psychic energy." He notes, in his book *Flow: The Psychology of Optimal Experience*, "We create ourselves by how we invest this energy." In other words, where you focus your attention dictates how rich or miserable your life is in that moment.

MEASURING PSYCHIC ENERGY

Biofeedback researchers have found evidence that "consciousness technology" works. Change your emotional state and mental focus, and you change yourself. Upbeat music counteracts sadness. Hypnotherapy and focused attention knit bones. Visualization wins championships. Paying attention to your attention improves your experience of life.

Recently, this research has turned "inside out." Not only does psychic energy affect how successfully we deal with challenges, but it also radiates out into the world. In the 1990s, researchers at the University of Arizona set out to identify the impact of this broadcasting. In a particularly fascinating study, two subjects stood in opposite corners of a room, their backs to each other. One subject looked at pictures that evoked various emotions; the other had nothing to look at. The brain activity of both was electronically monitored. Each time the first person registered measurements above the baseline, corresponding variations in mental activity showed up on the other person's monitor. In particular, sharp spikes of anger seemed to travel instantaneously from one to the other. The person deprived of visual stimuli could see neither the pictures nor the person looking at them. Nor could he hear the pages turning. Yet the monitors revealed a significant correlation between the emotional states of the two subjects.

Studies in quantum physics support this phenomenon, suggesting that forces we cannot see are in fact quantifiable. In other words, it's possible that we're constantly sensing energy transmitted by other people, and perhaps by objects as well. With this in mind, we need to trust the intuitions that arise in response to the transmissions of psychic energy.

Research findings pertaining to psychic energy lend credence to present-day attraction theories. New Age philosophers tell us that our intentions create reality. Positive thoughts attract positive experiences. Negative thoughts draw unwanted experiences. Believe in abundance and we attract wealth. Dwell on scarcity and we create impoverishment. We see, we judge, we fear, we expect ... we get.

Even more important, the studies indicate that our psychic energy is patterned not only on our responses to immediate events but also on our memories of past events. In fact, past influences are as powerful as present ones in impacting the energy we transmit, and hence the world we create. In the moment, you may think searching for a fabulous off-the-trail restaurant can turn a bland weekend into a grand adventure; however, if you're convinced that unknown eateries are unknown for good reason, you may bypass this option and suffer disappointment. What's more, everyone around you will feel your malaise.

The mind is a powerful tool. It can instantly destroy joy in a roomful of people.

OVERRULING YOUR MEMORIES

Memories hijack the mind, commanding us to engage in or avert emotionally laden experiences, and to express or suppress our feelings about them. Memories can fool us into thinking we are taking care of ourselves when in fact we're neither experiencing an event in the moment nor learning from it. They can trick us into thinking we're in control of a situation when actually we're pushing people away for fear that we'll lose control.

The good news is, you can regain command of your mind by becoming conscious of your choices. Despite feelings of disappointment, disillusionment, anxiety, anger, jealousy, shame, or guilt, you can choose to act however you'd like. Memories will always be running around in your head. But you can identify them, converse with them, detach from them, explore your choices while unencumbered by them, and select the most desirable course of action.

Aware of your choices, you are able to see beyond the expectations posed by disappointing memories. Your perception expands from *what you assume will happen* to an imagination of what else *could* happen. Choose to cruise. Choose to go for a walk rather than put in another hour of work. Choose to love your partner's melodic snoring instead tossing, turning, and cursing the roar. Choose to sing your way through traffic instead of raging at the other drivers. Choose to write an enlightening memoir instead of wallowing in pain. Assumptions of gloom lead to inaction. Unfulfilled dreams lead to heartache. Counteract your negative expectations by lifting your awareness from the horizontal world of the past to the vertical world of the present.

Any time you are upset or afraid, look for the frame you've placed around the situation. Then either widen your point of view to find more promising circumstances or disband the frame altogether, rendering your opinions and judgments powerless. Investing your psychic energy in untapped possibilities can override the power of an obstructing memory and put you back in charge of your life.

It's tough changing the channel from "what a drag" to "what a joy." But once you've done it, using the tips described below, you'll be released from the prison of negative expectations. The goal is to lighten up. No one can dance through life top-heavy.

Accept the Truth

You cannot be disillusioned unless you have an illusion. The moment you accept that you can't take your planned vacation, you're free to choose how to spend the time. The moment you recognize that all the people, circumstances, relationships, opportunities, challenges, and limitations in your life are real, you can choose to leave or stay, save or exchange them, add to or subtract from them, love them or lose them, redecorate or move on, or find a way to dignify what you have.

In changing channels, the first step is to give up resistance and denial. Quit wasting your time blaming people, machines, or the weather. Stop comparing yourself with others who have something you desperately want. You can't improve on what you have until you acknowledge its existence. It may not be fair that you were passed over for the promotion, that you gain weight just looking at food, that the person you love wants someone else, that your stock plummeted, or that you can no longer run around the block. You don't have to like what you see. But you have to say "hello" to it, shake hands with it, and go about your day with it by your side before deciding what to do about it.

There are days when I speak, write, and breathe with absolute joy. On other days, I fall back to earth. Last Valentine's Day, the man I called my boyfriend informed me by e-mail that he no longer wanted to see me because he was too tired to date. The following day, an article featuring my coaching practice got bumped from a national magazine's production schedule. Then a recurring infection recurred. By mid-afternoon, I was feeling unattractive, broken, and helpless. Eventually I told myself that if a man I'm dating can't talk to me directly, then he might not like me enough to work out relationship problems; I'll find someone who does. The magazine, I mused, missed a good story; there are other publications to pitch it to. Poor health, I admitted, mirrors back imbalances in my life; it's time to tune in and reflect. Although I didn't like these circumstances, I refused to let the pain, anger, and doubt destroy my entire day.

To cultivate acceptance, acknowledge your present reality, then expand the box. Verbalize your fears, hurts, embarrassment, or shame. Then add the word *and* to your statement. I am arrogant. *And* I am compassionate and loyal to my friends. I'm a lousy record-keeper. *And* I'm good at paying for the help I need. I'm jealous of my friend who's now a successful artist. *And* I'm happy for her good fortune, and eager to let her help me earn mine.

Recently, I was pleased to see Troy, a trainer at the local gym, return to work. He had lost his bid for world champion in a body-building tournament. Winning had been his dream for years. He had worked hard, modeling discipline and persistence. Another trainer feared Troy wouldn't be back. She said his defeat had been a major blow. The next day, Troy strutted into the gym as proud as I had ever seen him. Five people rushed over to greet him. Within minutes, his old buddies had him laughing. One by one, clients and acquaintances shook his hand, patted his shoulder, boxed his ear, or walked by and winked. Troy lost the tournament. And he is our hero.

Acceptance also means seeing the good in uncomfortable situations. The man who rejected me set me free to participate in a better relationship. The publisher started me on a quest for more harmonious vehicles for my story. And the infection sent me off to a doctor who recommended a more effective medication and dietary guidelines that not only boosted my resistance to future infections but also improved my overall well-being. Acceptance revved up my psychic energy and propelled me into motion, attracting more desirable circumstances.

A Sufi story tells of a father who was outside one night, crying loudly. His young son found him and said, "Father, why do you weep?"

"Alas, my son, I weep for you and your affliction."

"What affliction?" asked the boy.

"I'm sorry you were born with double vision."

"But father," said the boy, "I have no affliction." He pointed to the sky. "If I did, I'd see four moons up there."

Who is driving your train down the track? While in the grip of denial or resistance, you cannot be the engineer. But once you acknowledge the rocks and bumps on the tracks, you can grab the wheel and mastermind a more gratifying ride.

Break the Spell of Persistence

Many of us, from as far back as we can remember, have been advised to persist. Hard work and a never-give-up attitude, we were told, are the ingredients for success. The often repeated mantra was, "Keep your feet on the ground, nose to the grindstone, and never look back."

Yet for every person who champions willpower and determination, there is a counterpart who declares, "I worked so hard, but I now wish I had done something else." The truth is that while operating under the spell of persistence any one of us may persevere at joyless endeavors.

To overrule the memories that keep you trapped in disappointment, recognize that at times it is best to scrap a desire, a goal, or an entire vision. Yes, believe in the power of goals. Yet also understand that if the debris is extensive enough to topple your train, it's time to change tracks. When your child begs for attention, your ulcers scream for Mylanta, and your number one client tells you to "give it a rest," heed the signals.

A change of heart can save your heart. For best results, focus your psychic energy only on difficulties that you can alter. Let go of the others.

How do you know whether to dig in your heels or take flight? Try the exercise described in figure 7–1. If after completing this exercise you decide to give up a battle, understand that moving on is not a matter of giving up. Rather, it's a way of consciously shaping your most precious resources—your time, stamina, and power to create.

Figure 7–1

Energy Allocation Exercise

To evaluate how to expend your energy most productively when hard work is getting you nowhere, follow these ten steps. You just might discover that it's time to stop banging your head against the wall.

1. Divide a sheet of paper in half. Label the left side "Can't Control" and the right "Can Control," as is illustrated below.

Can't Control	Can Control

2. Think about the desire you cannot materialize. Under "can't control," list aspects of the situation that you're unable to change. Be honest with yourself. If you're trying to change someone's mind or behavior, and they haven't budged in months, it's safe to conclude that you're wasting your time. If you are, list the person's name, along with other uncontrollable factors, in this column.

3. Under "can control," list aspects of the situation that you could conceivably change. Include steps you'd be willing

to take in order to gain ground. This is not an exercise in fault-finding or blaming; it's an acknowledgment of the powers you would like to activate more fully.

Something you do or say may, after all, mitigate the situation. If your desire is to revise a policy, might you ask to attend a meeting and participate in a critical discussion, or can you phone in a suggested revision? Can you invite an unyielding coworker to lunch, where they may be more inclined to listen to your ideas? If you say, "I'm sorry," might you shift a loved one's point of view? Add to your "can control" column any effort that could make a difference, no matter how slight.

4. Returning to your "can't control" list, see if you can let go of the need to change any of these aspects. Place a check mark beside each one you honestly believe you can detach from.

5. Review your "can control" list. Which items are you currently working on? Are there any you can commit to initiating today? Place a check mark beside each item you are either working on or willing to activate immediately.

6. In the top left-hand quadrant of the diagram on page 144, list in pencil the "can't control" items that you *didn't* check off. These issues are your "dead horses." Regardless of how often you kick them, they won't stir. It can take time to bury a dead horse, but you'll feel better when it's over.

Instead of choosing to bury a dead horse on the spot, you may decide to continue kicking it, certain that persistence or a miracle will elicit change. If you opt for this approach, ensure that the battle supports your vision, then brace yourself for a long, hard struggle. Each day, remind yourself that you can choose something different tomorrow.

	Can't Control	Can Control
High A M O U N T O F E N E R G Y	*Dead Horses*	*Cool Cats*
	Freed Birds	*Sitting Ducks*

Low   DEGREE OF CONTROL   High

7. When the day comes that you can let go of a dead horse, erase the item and print it in the lower left-hand box, labeled "Freed Birds." Dead horses become freed birds when you deliberately release them from your life. And with each freed bird, you disengage from the struggle, liberating more of your energy. You free up your energy when you are finally able to let your mother's insensitive remarks roll off your back, or when you patiently accept that your client will call for help at the last minute. To release a dead horse, open your arms and let the difficulty fly away. Before you know it, the liberated energy will be better placed.

It's not easy to abandon a cause. Letting go of something you've deemed important may be one of the hardest things you'll ever do. To ease the hardship, remind yourself that trying to ride a dead horse in the name of justice will only cause you to lose ground in your relationship or career, and certainly in approaching your vision. Also take to heart the words of George Bernard Shaw, who said, "Those who cannot change their minds cannot change anything."

8. Now ask yourself, "Am I spending time on the items that are within my control?" Hopefully your answer will be "yes." To find out, go down your "can control" list, transferring the checked-off items—those you are working on or are about to tackle—to the "cool cats" box. Acknowledge yourself for the gains you're making.

9. Finally, place the "can control" items that you're doing *nothing* about in the "sitting ducks" box. How do you feel about these parts of your life? Most people who don't change what they can will experience themselves as victims continually subject to the domination of others. Victims see the world as unfair and uncontrollable. They become increasingly angry at those who "take away" their happiness. In short, they don't allow themselves to enjoy life.

   A Yiddish proverb proposes that "*no choice* is a choice too." Inaction, in other words, is a choice. For every item you've chosen not to act on, ask yourself why, and let your answers reveal the obstructions hiding within you. Job proclaimed, "When I defend myself, my own mouth defeats me." We tell ourselves, "I'm too short" or "My parents were thoughtless" or "I'm a member of a minority group"—all of which keep the soul from flourishing. Listen to your stories. Then tell your truth. Self-imposed barriers are the easiest ones to lift.

> 10. Budge ever so little, remembering that it takes only five minutes of bravery to be stronger today than you were yesterday. Then, one by one, take action to move the "sitting duck" items to the "cool cats" box. Again, acknowledge the gains you're making.

Practice this exercise regularly. Over time, you are bound to feel more inner power and less anger and frustration. Above all, don't revert to kicking dead horses. Keep your energy from leaking. A healthy supply of energy is needed to feel happy and powerfully in control of your life.

Know What Muddies Your Perception

What muddies your view of the present? Most often, the failure to notice possibilities in the here-and-now is not due to misperceptions. We miss the present because we *don't see* it. And we fail to see it because we've latched on to patterns of thinking and behaving that help us feel good or safe. These recurring thoughts and actions have become routines—unconscious rituals that inhibit free choice and prevent us from stepping fully into the joy of living. Our routines may bring us momentary pleasure. But in the end, they cause us unhappiness and stress.

Our most common routines are our attachments—to smoking, caffeine, sugar, relationship dramas, fixing other people's problems, and pursuing partnership to keep us from feeling alone. Actually, the intractable pursuit of *anything* can block us from seeing the glorious possibilities in our midst.

For example, some of my single women friends have listed the qualities they are looking for in a man. Although such lists help clarify their desires, they also present a "package" of traits that obliterates their view of the men currently in their world. The possibility of getting to know a wonderful man as a partner or friend becomes eclipsed by the judgments and opinions they're attached to.

How attached are you to preconceived notions? To determine your level of bondage to obstructing patterns of thought and behavior, complete the attachment index shown in figure 7–2.

FIGURE 7–2

Attachment Index

Rate each item on a scale of 1 to 5, with 1 representing "never," and 5 "always."

_____ Do you feel incomplete without an intimate relationship? Do your days have little meaning without a life partner? If you're dating, do you have a hard time concentrating on anything other than this person?

_____ Do you have sex regardless of the consequences, or when you don't really want to? Do you often think about sex? Do you avoid sex completely?

_____ Do you prioritize other people's needs over your own even when you are likely to suffer as a result? Do you spend a great deal of time thinking about other people's problems and how you might help?

_____ Are you always getting hurt? Do people step on you? Are you suffering?

_____ Do you smoke cigarettes to calm your nerves? Do you smoke more than one cigarette per day?

_____ Do you drink an alcoholic beverage every day?

_____ Do you regularly take drugs to feel good, to sleep, or to be entertained?

_____ Do you drink a caffeinated beverage every day?

_____ Do you consume sugar at least once a day?

_____ Are you routinely late for meetings and appointments? Do you frequently feel rushed?

_____ Are you easily upset? Do you hold on to these feelings for hours, maybe days?

_____ Do you keep eating after you're full? When you're working or relaxing, do you often think about your next meal?

_____ Do you watch television or videos for more than 10 hours a week?

_____ Do most of your conversations center on you?

_____ Do you stop in front of mirrors to check out your appearance?

_____ Do you shop for clothing, furniture, electronics, or cosmetics at least once a week?

_____ Do you work more than 50 hours a week?

_____ Do you often think about work while you're relaxing at home?

_____ Do you gamble more than twice a month?

_____ Do you have a hard time asking for help?

_____ Do you move on to new projects before completing earlier ones?

_____ Do you avoid certain types of people due to social class, cultural, religious, or sexual preferences?

_____ Do you have a hard time conversing with people in authority?

_____ Do you pay your bills late?

_____ Is money tight? Do you have little or no savings?

_____ Do you insist on getting your way?

_____ Are you always busy? Would it be difficult to do "nothing" for 1 hour?

_____ Do you have to be right? Do you have to be loved or adored? Do you have to be perfect?

_____ Do you see no way out of the life you are living?

As you review your responses, congratulate yourself on the items rated 1 or 2. Keep an eye on the 3's. Try not to give these behaviors more energy than you currently do; less would be better. Items marked 4 or 5 reflect areas of attachment that keep you from seeing alternatives. Detaching from these habits may require only a simple declaration, or it may call for months of working with a therapist, counselor, or personal coach. Starting with the 3's, set goals to decrease your habituation. Once you've reached these objectives, commit to freeing yourself from the 4's, then finally the 5's. In other words, begin to liberate your energy by peeling off the loosest restraints first. Then gradually proceed to those with a stronger grip.

Attachments imprison you. They block out light, limiting your choices by narrowing your field of observable possibilities. The less encumbered you are, the clearer your vision will be.

Keep Your Perspective Clear

While suspending expectations and judgments, releasing needs, and detaching from your patterns of thought and behavior, you clear the slate for creation. Life becomes a stage, with you as the director. The curtain rises. You see the entire picture. It is within your power to arrange the scenes, spotlight the major actors, decide how the story unfolds, and guide the outcome. If your choice is a joyous life, accept the present, focus on what you can change, then free yourself to be anything you desire.

The Danish philosopher Søren Kierkegaard said, "The most common despair . . . is not choosing or willing to be oneself." If you can't find joy within yourself, how will you find it elsewhere? You must *be* your joy, *be* your passion, *be* authentically you. Don't just eat. Taste the flavors. Don't just hear. Listen with your heart. Don't just see. Feel the colors and curves. Don't just touch. Absorb the temperatures and textures. Sample all the possibilities life has to offer.

Author Nancy Slonim Aronie says that when you open yourself up by abandoning your habitual ways of thinking for an hour or two, you become God's conduit for creativity. The clear pipelines, she adds, are the ones into which God pours "extreme love out there onto the desert." Surely, there are a million reasons for not nurturing yourself. You're too busy. You're too scared. You're ashamed of who you are.

You're overwhelmed. You're angry...*Stop!* Clap your hands. Snap your fingers. Shout, "No more!" as loud as you can. Then choose to think about something else, preferably something beautiful that is right under your nose. With that, you become a first-rate player in the possibility game.

The key to acting on possibilities is to recognize when you're drifting off into yesterday or tomorrow. Then do whatever it takes to reenter the present. Play music. Pinch yourself. Call a friend. Take a walk. Forgive yourself. Forgive those who have disappointed you. Plan a grand adventure within five miles of your home. Once you're back in action, remember who you are and the gifts you bear. You can't lose when you've chosen joy.

Part III

CAPTURE
THE RAPTURE

*Until our experience of the present
is intrinsically rewarding, we are hostages
held by a hypothetical future or a dead past.*

—Mihaly Csikszentmihalyi

When I ask people to describe their experiences of joy, they speak of winning competitions, triumphing over difficulties, laughing with their children, or lounging in the sun and smelling the fragrance of rosebushes they've pruned with their own hands. Deliciously, they detail their memories. Yet never has anyone defined joy as their experience of the present moment—the space we occupied as we talked.

Part III of this book will lead you across the threshold of time, space, and expectation to the discovery of joy within you from one moment to the next. Already you have learned to enter the vertical world. Using your power to create, you can claim your purpose, map out a vision, and begin to approach it. All that's left is to recognize that the joy you feel while bridging the gap is not an external or random experience likely to vanish when the going gets rough. At that point, you will have evolved from doing things that make you happy to being a person delighted by life. Whether you are on the job or vacationing, with strangers or with family, your existence can indeed be rooted in love, inspiration, and compassion.

Getting there, however, may not be easy. For one thing, it calls for disciplining the heart as well as the mind. How will you know when your heart is well-disciplined? You will wake up each morning feeling love and gratitude—emotions that you can continue to draw from until the day's end. As miraculous as this may sound, capturing your rapture is not an act of God. It's the result of practice, each day of which can bring you increased buoyancy.

Another reason for the difficulty in embracing joy is that removing the final frames of the horizontal world can be frightening. After all, they form the protective boundaries within which we've been living. At the same time, they reflect back to us images imprinted with trauma that define us in our most miserable, victimized states. These freeze-frames give us reasons for rationalizing our unhappiness. For example, a forty-five-year-old man named Jack recently told me his workaholism and problematic relationships were rooted in early childhood: when Jack was two days old, his father left home, and ever afterward his mother blamed the family's breakup on Jack's birth. Fixated on his misfortune, Jack feels justified in avoiding intimacy.

Breaking out of the horizontal world is doubly frightening because it forces us to part with comfortable routines. According to sociologist Robert Snow, PhD, routines calm our bodies and comfort our minds. No doubt, but they also numb us to the present moment, as we saw in chapter 7. While grumbling about the late delivery of the morning paper, we fail to notice the migrant cardinal in the tree or the bee flying into its new hive tucked into the eaves of the house. Those of us who have managed to let go of the past often end up clinging to the future and getting lost in recurring fantasies of soulmates, fame, or fortune. Life passes us by when we focus our energy on thoughts of what we've lost or worry about losing, or on what we don't have or think we should have.

How do you transcend this joyless past-future continuum? By pushing your way out, forcing your mind into the present moment. Jump—you won't need a safety net. Leap for the thrill of it. The leap will get easier each time you do it.

The five chapters that follow will help you break through to joy over and over again. You'll start by opening your mind to the present moment. Once anchored in the present, you'll learn to fuse your mind with your vision. In the end, you'll know how to be your radiant, joyful self at work, at play, and in love.

CHAPTER 8

Basking in the Present

*When I get that feeling
of quiet and obliviousness
within myself, I feel I can't lose.*

—Jane Blalock

We humans are masters at zoning out. While someone is speaking to us, we can smile, nod, say "uh-huh" and "hmm," and still wonder if the front door is locked, plan dinner, and rehearse our reply for when the person finally takes a breath. While on the phone, we can inspect the lock on the door, inventory the food available for dinner, and clear out our e-mail message box. Amidst it all, one or two of the speaker's words may land in our consciousness, enabling us to dart into the present moment just long enough to keep the conversation going.

We can zone out practically anywhere and still survive. We become incognizant of our surroundings while concentrating deeply, watching television, or driving. Indeed, how many other drivers do you suppose are operating on automatic pilot? Think about this question the next time you refuse to fasten your seat belt.

The Internet operates in reverse. While logging on, we zone into cyberspace, lost to the world around us. Although surfing the Net may appear synonymous with being in the zone, it is not, for it numbs our emotions instead of sparking them.

The Internet snared me the first month I signed on. I furiously answered my e-mail, made airline reservations, and shopped for everything I might need in the coming decade. Thoroughly engaged, I was miles from my body. Only after turning off the computer did I feel my discomfort. By then, my back ached miserably, my eyes burned, and my mouth was so dry I couldn't spit.

One morning, aware that a client would be calling in about five minutes, I turned on the computer. I vowed that I would not read my e-mail but would simply see how many messages were waiting for a reply, which would help me plan the day. My cat, PK, crawled into my lap. I let her settle in even though I knew I'd soon be getting up.

When I clicked on "New Mail," the screen filled with addresses. I complained inwardly about my lack of time, the shackle of work I had created, and the people who had nothing better to do than send jokes and chain letters. Surely, I had a few minutes to begin chipping away at the daunting list of messages that awaited me. I decided to read one or two, maybe three.

PK, meanwhile, was stretching, as cats do. After extending a leg toward the ceiling, she slowly lowered it to the keyboard, resting her paw on the "Delete" key. Within seconds, the screen had cleared. And, following a momentary panic, so had my mind. I turned off the computer, made myself a cup of tea, and curled up on the couch, peacefully awaiting my client's call. Our conversation was magical. I detected more meaning in her words, her tone, and her silences than I had in previous discussions. She declared me a wizard among coaches. I didn't tell her that I had just been jolted into the present by a far better coach—my cat.

Although the present moment holds sweet rewards, we often need help getting there. Overcoming decades of mental conditioning that blocks out the present, trapping our attention in the past or future, takes discipline, persistence, and practice—behaviors rarely associated with happiness. Yet the return on this investment is huge. Assistance is available through the techniques described on the following pages.

THE PRESHOT PROCEDURE

Did you know that the warm-up practices performed by professional athletes help them stay present during competitions? Baseball players step up to the plate and swing the bat three times before positioning themselves. If the pitcher waits too long to release the ball, they'll repeat the movements. Basketball players standing at the free-throw line execute a series of movements such as bouncing the ball, mouthing mantras, and pulling their ear lobes before shooting for the basket. If they feel distracted or off center, they'll stop partway through their ritual and start over. Golfers maintain a certain pace as they walk toward the ball, then they complete a "preshot procedure" before swinging. One pro told me that if she ever started toward the tee with her left foot instead of her right, she would return her club to the bag and begin again. I asked her if she was superstitious. "No," she said, "it's just that replicating the same steps and rhythms helps me feel centered and in harmony with the present moment."

The techniques used by athletes can help you remain present to your life. Any time you catch yourself contemplating the past, fearing the future, or worrying about how others will judge you, you can deliberately alter your state of mind by embarking on a practice that works for you.

A good starting point is the following rendition of the preshot procedure used by golfers. This practice consists of four steps: relax, detach, center, and focus.

Relax

Begin by relaxing your body. Tight muscles restrict blood flow to the brain. When blood flow is restricted, powerful emotions overrule logical thoughts, subjecting human behavior to a series of physiological responses. Daniel Goleman, author of *Emotional Intelligence,* cites several physiological responses to emotional states. Here are some of them:

- Anger directs blood to the hands, preparing the person to strike.

- Fear directs blood to the large muscles, mostly in the legs, preparing the person to flee.

- Sadness and disappointment decrease the metabolic rate, giving the person time to adjust to loss.

- Happiness directs blood to the brain, quieting worrisome thoughts, freeing up energy, and releasing overall good feelings.

Of these emotions, only happiness maximizes blood flow to the brain. With a fully activated brain, you can avail yourself of logic, see more possibilities, and make better decisions. Therefore, to activate your brain while faced with anger, fear, pressure, or physical stress, you must first calm your body.

There are many ways to relax. Try counting backward from one hundred to one, flicking your wrists to shake out tension, or taking three long, slow breaths. For ongoing effects, deliberately slow down your life. Eat slowly, drive leisurely, walk at a gentle pace.

When pressures mount and you feel the adrenaline coursing through your veins, say, "I quit," and change your activity. Take a walk, ask a stranger how their day is going, send a card to a friend, talk to an animal, hug a loved one, or simply close your eyes and give thanks for being alive. If you're in the midst of a conversation or a meeting, stop, breathe deeply, and send your mind to a "happy place." Burn victims are taught to overcome pain by journeying to such a place. My "happy place" is on the soft couch in my living room, looking out at the blue Arizona sky. No matter where I am, I can close my eyes and "go home."

I learned another relaxation technique from my grandmother Jenny, whom I called Bubby. She escaped from Russia with her husband during the Bolshevik Revolution. Only fourteen years old at the time, she never again heard from her parents or her three sisters.

After my grandfather died, I spent many weekends with Bubby. On Friday evenings, after lighting the Sabbath candles, she would stare into the flames for the longest time. Finally, she'd close her eyes, sway to a tune she heard in her head, and smile. Opening her eyes, she'd look at me and say, "My family is well. We danced and sang. My sisters and I braided each other's hair. Come, let me show you." Then, by the light of the candles, Bubby would teach me Russian folk songs while braiding my hair.

Bubby didn't dwell on her losses. Instead, she used her fondest memories to help her find peace in the present. Now, twenty-one years after her death, I combat fear and loneliness by lighting a candle, gazing into the flame, and hearing her sweetly singing.

Relaxing also releases the need to control, increasing the energy flow through the body. When you relinquish the need to be in charge of a situation, possibilities appear. Magic happens.

While touring the jungles of northern Thailand, I traveled part of the way by elephant. For the first half of the trek, I rode on the platform and the *mahout,* my guide, rode on the young elephant's head. An hour into the jungle, the *mahout* opted to walk, whereupon I asked if I could take his place on the animal's head. He gestured for me to move up.

Fancying myself the Queen of the Jungle, I beat my chest and howled to the trees. As we headed up a steep hill, I leaned back to maintain my balance. When we reached the summit, I relaxed and congratulated myself for being such a skillful rider.

The celebration was premature. Instead of walking along the ridge, the elephant headed straight down the mountainside. Falling forward, I grabbed for her hair, only to find that young elephants have no hair. Her head was too big to envelop with my arms. My legs were equally useless. Although I clenched my calves and thighs, hoping to stick to her like glue, within minutes my muscles ached. I knew I couldn't hold on much longer.

Glancing up, I saw a tree. Immediately, I formulated a plan: using what little strength I had left, I'd swing off and out of the way of the creature's bone-crushing feet. Reaching up, I released the tension in my legs. At that moment, the elephant wrapped her ears around my calves, pinning my legs securely to her head. I relaxed and surrendered control to her. For the rest of the trip, I happily rode up and down the hills.

Relinquishing the need to control works as well in business as it does on elephants. Periodically, I face a dry spell in my coaching business. Clients move on and new prospects slow to a trickle. My all-too-human mind reacts. I frantically ransack my Rolodex, all the while declaring myself a failure. Then my trained mind kicks in. I stretch out on the couch, let my cat crawl into my lap, and thank God for creating the space for miracles to happen. Or I take myself to a movie, or invite a friend to a sushi bar, or the zoo, or an animal shelter for an hour of petting. Within days, my phone invariably rings, promising new business opportunities.

A state of relaxation also invites new partnerships. Many single women and men meet wonderful partners after vanquishing their loneliness by deciding to have fun. Laughing people, after all, are far more appealing than sulking ones.

Whatever it is you are looking for, there's no need to cling desperately to elephant heads or mope around in a cloud of gloom. Your best bet is to relax and lighten up. You'll be amazed at the response.

Detach

The next step in the preshot procedure is to detach from problems and worries by emptying your brain. Cleaning out the clutter—worries about work, money troubles, rough relationships, and unresolved arguments—makes space for joy to enter. Golf great Jane Blalock calls this technique the art of "obliviousness." To practice obliviousness, let your thoughts float away. If they're reluctant to fly, ask them to slip out for a while. If you practice this clearing technique for one minute, then three minutes, then five, and gradually longer, you will be able to send your thoughts on an extended vacation. You can invite them back later if need be.

What are our weightiest thoughts? Among those that confuse and control us the most are the judgments we form about situations in our world. As Stoic philosopher Epictetus said nearly 2,000 years ago, "Man is disturbed not by events that happen, but by his opinion of events that happen." Of equal bearing are our concerns regarding the opinions others form about us. And yet, as acting coach Gary Austen insists, "it's none of your business what people think of you. It's your business to be in your body, acting your passion and being your joy. If you do that, [everyone around you] will join you for the ride." Detach from your ponderous thoughts and you will experience peace of mind—emptiness, silence, obliviousness.

I learned the power of detaching the first time I spoke at a conference. Working toward my master's degree in broadcasting, I was studying an unconventional use of video. I had found that showing people videotapes of themselves talking could, over time, elevate their self-esteem. I was testing my theories on drug addicts and prison inmates. I chose the capital of unconventional thought, San Francisco, as the home base for my work, eventually applying the findings with the help of therapists at the Haight Ashbury Free Medical Clinic.

One day, the clinic's medical director encouraged me to speak at the annual conference of the American Psychological Association, to be held in Los Angeles. I refused, claiming I was unqualified.

"Your work is revolutionary," he said. "It can't hurt to try."

So I filled out the forms and mailed them in. Two months later, I received an invitation to spend twenty minutes, along with two other speakers, discussing the uses of video in therapy. The session, although scheduled as a breakout meeting, was given a prominent spot on the first day's agenda. I gathered reams of research, edited a sample video, colored a set of overheads, and wrote and rewrote a knock-'em-dead speech.

The day before my planned drive to the conference, I received a call from a woman named Glennis.

"Ms. Reynolds," she said in a high-pitched voice, "some items seem to be missing from your application. I'm responsible for introducing you. I need to know where you received your PhD."

My heart sunk. "I don't have one," I said sheepishly.

"Oh," she replied. "Then please tell me where you are a candidate for your doctorate."

"I'm not."

"Oh." A thick silence spread between us before she added, "Then please tell me you have, or nearly have, a master's degree in a relevant field."

I could barely form an answer. "My degree will be in broadcasting."

"It's too late to change the agenda," Glennis said. "Come if you want." Then she hung up.

Little gremlins danced through my head singing, "We told you so. You're not good enough." Their cousins chimed in with, "They'll laugh at you, ignore you, throw you out on your ear."

Had I not been twenty-four years old and relatively inexperienced in failure, I might have let my brain get the best of me. As it was, I awoke early the next morning and threw the research, video, colored overheads, and presentation into the backseat of the car. While heading down Highway 5, I sang along with Tina Turner, drowning out the voices in my head.

The Bonaventure, an awesome hotel, looked like a steel-and-glass castle. The moment I stepped into the ballroom, it was apparent that thousands of people had arrived for the conference. I found the registration desk, filled out the necessary forms, and smiled as a woman handed me a name tag and speaker's ribbon, informing me that my session was scheduled for the hour before lunch. Sporting my ribbon, I strutted back into the ballroom.

The morning passed slowly. When it came time for the breakout session, a woman silenced the crowd and then introduced the first speaker. Mentally practicing my presentation, I barely heard him. Then a different woman introduced the second speaker. This time I tried to pay attention but was too nervous to get anything more than the gist of her message. Finally, a third introducer stood up and faced the audience. After glancing at her watch, she spoke in a high-pitched voice—and I knew in a flash it was Glennis. "We're running a bit behind. I know you don't want to be late for lunch. The next speaker informed me that she didn't have time to fully prepare. If you'd prefer to go to lunch, you may leave."

I tried not to notice that the room was clearing as I made my way to the podium. I cued up my video, stacked my research, aligned my first overhead slide, and swallowed hard. Looking up, I saw only one person in the room. He crossed his arms and said, "I'm not all that hungry. Why don't you go ahead."

Have you ever had a deciding moment where you could have just as easily fled the scene than to stay and make a fool out of yourself? I chose to stay. In so choosing, I took a quick self-study course in detachment.

I introduced myself, then launched into my presentation. I described the research, showed the video, and displayed the overheads, offering the audience of one everything I had.

When I finished, he gave me a standing ovation and handed me his card. "Use me as a reference any time you want," he said kindly.

Was he a world-renowned psychologist? Probably not. Nevertheless, months later, while compiling a résumé for my first job application, I asked him for a letter of recommendation. It was his letter that won me a staff position at a mental hospital.

The moral of the story is this: Detach from past humiliation, release all thoughts of future outcomes, and give 100 percent to the moment. The divine plan will unfold in due course.

The paradox is that to control your mind you have to empty it. You set the cruise control and release the wheel. You don't know where you'll end up; you just know it will be the right place. And provided that you have nothing to lose, you'll most likely do your best. You'll sink your longest putt, deliver a top-notch speech, meet the mate of your dreams. Why? Because in eradicating past and future, fears and hopes, as well as disappointments and expectations, you're free to plunge into the present. This is where you'll see extraordinary results. This is where you'll achieve mastery.

Olympic champion sprinter Michael Johnson says that although crossing the finish line feels great, the real thrill comes at the start of the race, when you're in the moment. That's when your mind, unconcerned about end results, competitors, or the passage of time, is focused on the experience itself. If there's nothing going on in your head to divert you, every fiber of your being is woven into the here and now. The challenge, Johnson says, is to maintain this presence until the experience is over and it's time to celebrate.

While overreacting, blaming, worrying, or brooding, begin to detach by noticing the hook that is pulling you out of the here-and-now. Most likely, you will find that a need is clouding your mind. (For assistance, reread the needs list on page 43.) Once you've identified the culprit, visualize a big yellow balloon, stuff the need into the balloon, and let it sail out of your mind. For enduring results, watch it fly away.

If you have a long history with this need and are unable to let go of it completely, at least "park" it for an hour—gradually working up to two hours, then four, then more. Sooner or later, you'll be able to send this need, as well as other tenacious ones, on an extended vacation. In effect, detach from your needs or they'll sabotage your life.

Here's how detachment works for me. When I'm talking to a friend and my need to be right shows up, I say hello to it, stuff it into a balloon, and let it fly. Then, if I choose to, I say what was on my mind *behind* the need, such as explaining to my friend that I don't feel heard or that I'd like her to acknowledge my ideas even if she doesn't agree with them. In this way, I become more powerful than my needs.

Once you are able to relax your body and detach from your thoughts and needs, you'll be prepared to find peace, even joy, in the present. The next two steps will help you stay in this delightful state.

Center

"*Instincts* never lie." "Trust your *gut*." "Listen to the *voice* deep inside you." These are some of the many aphorisms that point to a well of wisdom and mindfulness beyond the bounds of the brain. Indeed, according to many traditions, the true center of the mind lies in the center of the *body*. To get there, you move your awareness out of your head and into your core—an act known as centering.

Where is your core? Some people say it's your heart. Others claim that the human core is more a feeling than a particular place. Performers and martial artists think of it as a central point just below the navel.

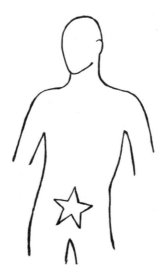

To find your central point, inhale deeply. Then move your attention to your heart or to the spot below your navel where the breath most fills your abdomen. While exhaling, keep your awareness on this spot. Let it settle there for a minute as you become familiar with this part of yourself.

With your awareness directed to this central point, scan your body to see what you can learn about your present state of being. Notice the feelings in your stomach. Do you detect hunger, discomfort, satiation? Pay attention to your legs. How do they feel? How about your toes? Check in with your fingers, your neck, and your hairline. Don't think—just feel. Notice sensations arising everywhere, from the cuticles of your toenails to the hair follicles on your scalp.

Sports psychologist Tom Kubistant, PhD, calls this activity *immersing*. He asks golfers to move into themselves by releasing all thoughts, tensions, and distractions, and to imagine themselves taking an elevator ride down the interior of their bodies. Following his guidelines, they eventually settle into deeper levels of themselves— where their true talents lie.

Once you are comfortable keeping your awareness out of your head and at your center, add a variety of activities to your practice. Play sports, or try reading, listening to music, or hiking. From this new perspective, you'll begin to see more details and hear finer nuances. Also take centering to work with you, and into your social interactions. It will enhance your rapport with others. Better yet, every day will be a fresh adventure brimming with receptivity and connectedness to the present moment.

Unfortunately, some people are afraid to center. Fearful of relinquishing the problem-solving brain activity they are accustomed to, they remain trapped in a pleasureless world of shoulds, can'ts, do's, and don'ts. If you, on the other hand, are willing to trade in security for pleasure, then break out of your mental prison by sending your awareness to the center of your body. Every skill you've ever learned will remain accessible while you're centering.

As with all new mental habits, centering requires daily practice. Give yourself time to master it, without "pushing the river," since the harder you *try* to center, the less effective your efforts will be. Simply sit back and let it happen.

If you're not one to sit back, try the "what if" method. Ask yourself, "What if I could be centered? What would it look like? What would it feel like?" Then walk through your house for three to five minutes at least twice a day, noticing as many details as possible and thinking only, "Centering would feel like this." Practice daily until your "what if" starts to feel like a natural experience. At that point, centering will be developing into a habit you won't have to think about. You'll soon be operating for hours each day from your center, fully aware that your body and mind can work happily in unison.

Focus

The fourth step in the preshot procedure is optional. If you can relax, empty your mind, and keep it clear and receptive, you'll have no trouble basking in the present. If you're like me, however, and thoughts have a way of hijacking your brain no matter what you do, your brain may need a focal point. For example, before a speaking engagement, I often write the word *fun* on a small piece of paper to set within my range of vision during the speech. If I'm committed to having fun, the audience too will enjoy themselves.

For other occasions I'll focus on the word *compassion*. Once, while I was complaining about my tyrannical boss, a spiritual therapist suggested I practice compassion and model the benefits of having a bright inner light. Reluctantly, I took her advice. During a difficult conversation with my boss, I focused on patience. To my surprise and delight, not only did he begin to hear—and appreciate—my ideas, but I was able to see how an understanding of his perspective could benefit me. As a result, we shifted from flexing our muscles at each other to showing respect.

One of my favorite focusing phrases is "Have a love affair with the moment." When I concentrate on the blazing love affair I am having with life, I'll hug a tree, sing to the stars, and smile at strangers with reckless abandon. In turn, life loves me back—unconditionally. The wind caresses my shoulders. Birds serenade me. My house holds me in its strong arms, protecting me from the cold.

There are countless ways to behave "on purpose" while zeroing in on the present. To intensify your concentration on a complex project for a period of time each day, try focusing on a vision of the outcome. To remember to think out of the box, expanding beyond current definitions and boundaries, focus on the word *creativity*. Whatever your objective might be, each extraneous thought that penetrates your brain is apt to decrease your effectiveness. To eliminate "wind drag" of this sort, work with the exercise described in figure 8–1.

FIGURE 8–1

Theme of the Month

Preselected themes can help anchor your brain any time you want to maintain a focused state. Since who you "be" is evolving over time, regard this focusing exercise as a lifelong practice.

- While sitting in a quiet spot, think of people you admire.

- Identify 12 qualities these people possess that you would like to demonstrate more often at work, at home, and with friends. Consider such traits as equanimity, authenticity, determination, courage, dedication, and spontaneity.

- Choose one trait to focus on for the next 30 days. To remember your theme for the month, record the word on several pieces of paper and tape them in strategic places such as on your phone, computer, appointment book, bedside table, and the dashboard of your car.

- The next time you are engaged in a conversation, adopt this theme as your focal point.

- After a month of working with this theme, select a new one.

- At the end of 12 months, celebrate your progress and take a month off. Then repeat this exercise, selecting 12 themes for the coming year, including any earlier ones you would like to give more focus to.

ATTENDING TO THE PRESENT

Attending to the present moment takes courage and patience, especially while trying to overcome a lifetime of distracting mental habits. If patience has not been your forté, remind yourself that there are many aspects of life you have not yet seen. Keeping your attention anchored in the present will create within you a welcoming arena for new ideas and viewpoints. Yes, you must trust that you will know what to do and say without thinking. This "standing in the unknowing" can be scary. It can also be magical. Not only will you see so much more, you'll also find that you are wiser and more capable than you ever imagined.

The following three disciplines can help you shift into the present at will. Practice them often. Before long, you will discover that being in the present is one of the simplest and most pleasurable gifts you can give yourself.

See Like a Poet

Poets have a knack for seeing exquisite, even sacred, details in the most mundane aspects of life. As a result, they come to know land-scapes, objects, and people intimately, whether viewing them for the first time or the hundredth. Hence seeing like a poet means giving your eyes permission to be curious—letting them feel and taste your surroundings. Revel in the colors, sizes, shapes, and textures you see; then close your eyes and absorb the scents.

When you see like a poet, you don't need to be standing on the shores of the Atlantic Ocean or at the base of the Himalayas to wit-ness grandeur. You can find beauty in the produce bins at the grocery store. The next time you shop, for instance, caress the soft fuzz of a peach, stroke a smooth-skinned eggplant, and pat a broccoli floret as if it were the head of a child. Look for dewdrops on the lettuce. Find the fattest tomato in the store. Hold a bunch of grapes up to the light and examine the thickness of their skins. Smell the melons. Count the varieties of apples. Congratulate the orangest orange and yellowest lemon. Squinting, scan the produce department, taking in the luscious reds, subdued whites, vivid greens, and bright yellows. Then breathe in the fresh scents as if inhaling steam from a pot of homemade soup.

My college photography professor taught me to see beauty in details when he had our class take rolls of black-and-white photographs on tiny parcels of land. Our instructions were to stand in one spot and shoot pictures of the square foot of ground around us, choosing any angle and distance. We had to keep the camera lens focused within the square-foot boundary even if it meant shooting twelve pictures of the same blade of grass. We were allowed one roll per stance. Then, switching to a new roll, we could move on to another location.

Confined to a small area of my backyard, I was amazed by many subtleties I would have otherwise missed. I noticed things I'd never before paid attention to, such as deep green moss on bark and tiny purple flowers I'd previously stepped on. I now shudder at the thought of accidentally crushing a gem that might not spring back in all its loveliness.

When you scrutinize the world around you, boredom dissipates and empty moments become endless treasures. Suddenly you can marvel over ants at work, marching into and out of a crack in the sidewalk. To flourish from these and other poetic experiences, practice the following exercise.

FIGURE 8–2

Awaken the Bard

To awaken the bard in your soul, work with this exercise for at least 5 minutes a day. Within a few weeks, your senses will be so heightened that you'll be delighting in the feast of life.

- **Stop everything.** Stand, sit, or lie in a comfortable spot indoors or out. Inhaling deeply, open your eyes wide, perk up your ears, free your hands, and part your lips to let your tongue taste the air as it travels inward.

- **Zoom in.** Narrow your focus to an area in front of you, preferably within two feet of your body. The closer, the better.

- **Absorb.** Explore the spot with all your senses, including touch. Allow your mind and emotions to respond randomly as the essence of each detail moves into and through your body. Free associate, comparing and contrasting the details with other landscapes, objects, or people you know. Allow memories to drift in and out of your consciousness, all the while maintaining contact with the present.

- **Merge.** Exploring the scene from other vantage points, notice similarities and differences between the various perspectives. Look at the spot upside down, then from the inside out. Merging the observer (you) with the observed (the scene), behold yourself as an integral part of the scene. Allow this world to be the only one that exists. You are the center, the pillar. The world lights up around you.

- **Record.** Pretend that you have been appointed the chronicler in charge of capturing these details for future generations. How would you describe what you see? Recite the words out loud. Write them down, if you wish, so that they may be shared with your own future generations.

Act Like a Child

One day I received an e-mail solicitation to join the Society of Childlike Grown-Ups. Their motto: "It's never too late to have a happy childhood, and to make sure that others do, too." Membership required a willingness to talk to animals, play under the bedcovers, and make a new friend each day. In addition, I would have to climb trees, take naps, and jump in puddles while walking in the rain. If I fell down, I had to bounce up laughing. If I hurt myself, I had to cry out loud until I was distracted by a stranger, a bright flower, or a twinkling star. I had to allow myself to feel scared, mad, or happy whenever these feelings showed up. I also had to act silly on impulse, and to kiss my mother, father, brothers, sisters, and friends no matter who was watching. In return, I would be officially authorized to frequent amusement parks, picnic areas, sandboxes, playgrounds, roller rinks, summer camps, circuses, ice cream parlors, aquariums, zoos, toy stores, and other gathering places for children of all ages. To remain a member in good standing, I had to play every day.

Like enrolling in the Society of Childlike Grown-Ups, entering the vertical world of presence requires us to play with reckless abandon—unhampered by senseless rules, incognizant of worries, and unhindered by feelings of embarrassment. Here we do not fret about anyone's opinions.

Nor do we cringe at the thought of someone witnessing our blunders. Instead, we act refreshingly ridiculous. We run to the mailbox, dance in the street, and love with all our hearts.

All that is required to act like a child is a shift in perspective—from "what" you are doing to "who" who are being. Instead of planning joyful activities, strive to be joy. As Tony Robbins, author of *Awake the Giant Within*, says, "In the end, all we have is who we become." To return to the blissful state of early childhood, lighten up, following the guidelines in figure 8–3.

FIGURE 8–3

Lighten Up Your Being

If your life has become so burdensome that you've forgotten how to play, practice these steps. Return to them any time you want to free your soul to fly.

- With paper and pen, sit comfortably in a quiet place where you're not likely to be disturbed. Close your eyes and picture yourself as who you want to be. *What are you doing?* Now see yourself acting this way at work, at home, and in your everyday encounters.

- Open your eyes and list everything you saw yourself doing. Add other activities you'd love to do. Include everything from playing with clay to swimming naked at noon.

- For each activity on your list, ask yourself three questions: "Who will I be if I do this?" "How will I feel if I do this?" and "What will I say about myself if I do this?" For instance, ask yourself who you would be if every once in a while you jumped out of bed and tinkered at your favorite hobby for half an hour before breakfast. How would you feel? What would you say about yourself if you spent your breaks at

---

work watching a caterpillar wriggle in the grass? Who would you be if you told your friends you love them?

- Review your answers. If the pictures entice you, plan on bringing them to life. Playfulness breaks through the chains of self-limitation. With joy, comes the freedom to be your true and happy self.

To lighten up and live in the vertical world, release the "elf" in your "self" so that your greatest pleasures—running with your dog, marveling at spring's first buds, or wrestling with your child—form the fabric of your everyday existence. I keep talking bears, Slinkys, rubber duckies, and other toys around my house. Seeing them, I cannot help but smile. I've also got a collection of Marx Brothers movies to watch when work has thrown me off balance. While driving, I often listen to *Charlotte's Web* or other children's books on tape. I no longer race around town for the sake of saving five minutes. In the words of the wise pig, Wilbur, "The world is a wonderful place when you're young."

There is no simpler way to learn to stay present than by acting like a child. Sing, even if you can't carry a tune. Dance without knowing the steps. Love without fearing the pain. You'll get more "smileage" out of life.

Approach Life with a Beginner's Mind
Zen master Suzuki Roshi said, "In the beginner's mind, there are many opportunities. In the expert's mind, there are none." How often do you put blinders on for purposes of being an expert, being right, or convincing yourself you know everything that's necessary? The better able you are to approach life with a beginner's mind, the more likely you will be to remove these last fragments of opinions and judgments that obstruct your view of possibilities in the moment.

I first learned of the Zen principle known as beginner's mind while working in Asia. Simply put, beginner's mind is the art of looking out on the world—people, places, and events—as if you've never seen them before. However, since everything in Asia was new to my senses, I couldn't put this practice to the test until I returned home.

Gloria, a Taiwanese colleague, returned with me. It was a mid-December evening. I was driving her from the airport to her hotel. As we inched along through traffic, I complained about having to work the next day while still feeling jet-lagged. Seconds later, Gloria started to scream. Much to my surprise, her face was radiant with delight as she pointed out the window. All I could see were houses. Then it hit: she was pointing at Christmas lights! Never before had she seen Christmas lights hung on houses.

I made a U-turn and headed for a street I knew would be festive with displays. As Gloria excitedly took photographs to show off back home, I mentally viewed the scene through her eyes. Ever so briefly, I too could revel in Christmas lights for the very first time.

Pleased with this technique, I practiced beginner's mind for the next few days. With fresh eyes, I relished in the graceful flight of a bird, the gentle opening of a flower, and the erratic jump of a grasshopper. Mastering this skill is easy, I decided, especially while looking at things I like.

While observing people, places, and events I did not particularly like, the practice proved to be quite difficult. Yet therein lay its magic.

My first magic lesson occurred with my cousin Stuart. I didn't know Stuart well. He grew up in Cleveland, Ohio, far from my home in Phoenix, Arizona. Although he seemed a nice enough guy, his whiny, slow-paced voice irritated me so much that I habitually ended our phone conversations as soon as I could.

A few years ago, the manufacturing company Stuart worked for transferred him to Douglas, Arizona. He called to tell me of the move and of his promotion to plant manager. I congratulated him and said I'd visit someday. Given the five-hour drive from Phoenix to Douglas, I could graciously find excuses *not* to visit. Consequently, I missed his marriage to a woman he met in Mexico and the birth of his three children.

One day, Stuart called to say, "Marcia, I've been transferred to a plant outside of Phoenix. My family can't come for about three months. I'm all alone. Can we go to dinner?"

Guilt got the best of me. The following Tuesday evening, I was sitting in a Chinese restaurant across the table from my cousin Stuart.

When he was midway into his fourth sentence, I thought, "Here it is—my opportunity to practice beginner's mind." I vowed to listen to Stuart as if I had never heard him before. I also decided to uncover something wonderful about him.

I listened. He droned on and on. My self-appointed mission grew more tedious as the minutes passed. Finally, the waitress's appearance saved the day. Yet before I could order, Stuart looked at her and said a few words in Chinese. At first, I was impressed. But seeing the look of confusion on the waitress's face, I immediately began to wonder how long the evening would last.

Then Stuart said, "Oh, you must not speak Mandarin. You must speak Cantonese." He then spoke to her in Cantonese. This time, she smiled and replied.

Amazed, I said, "Stuart, I know you speak Spanish. And from my travels, I've learned that people who speak Mandarin rarely speak Cantonese. You must have studied quite a few languages in college."

He said, "Oh no, not in college. I run factories. People come from all over. I just listen and pick up their language."

I did indeed find something wonderful about Stuart. At that point, his whine miraculously transformed into a singsongy cadence. Stuart, no longer a bore, turned into a fascinating person. I wanted to hear his stories. I found I enjoyed listening to cousin Stuart after all.

How many people have you blocked out of your life by erecting a wall of judgments and opinions? How many friends, coworkers, and relatives do you react to based on behavior they displayed months, if not years, ago? What foods or activities do you avoid because of unpleasant memories? What parts of your job do you dodge based on past disappointments? What parts of *yourself* do you circumvent? There is so much more to any person, place, and event than our minds typically allow us to see.

To enlarge your current perspective, remember that any time you observe a person, place, or event, you have two choices, as is diagrammed in figure 8–4: you can either clear your mind and see with fresh eyes, or frame the picture in past perceptions. If you look through a filter of old judgments and opinions, you'll be stuck in the past. Instead, observe with a beginner's mind and revel in a world vibrant with possibility.

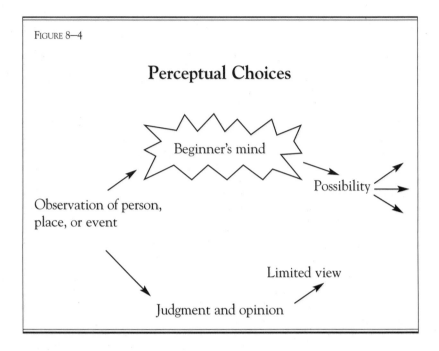

FIGURE 8—4

Perceptual Choices

Beginner's mind

Possibility

Observation of person, place, or event

Limited view

Judgment and opinion

As radio commentator Paul Harvey says, here is the "rest of the story." A year ago, toxic gas entered Stuart's house while he slept. He died before the problem was discovered.

I went to the funeral. There I recognized family members I'd seen only in photographs Stuart had shown me. Afterward, I went to his home, where I stood up and told the family about our night at the restaurant. They all laughed and thanked me for sharing the story. But before I could sit down, his mother said, "Let me tell you some other fabulous things about Stuart. Did you know he loved music? He wrote folk songs and symphonies although he never took a lesson. And he loved poetry. He wrote lyrics for many of his songs. And did you know he changed his religion? I wasn't too happy about that . . . until the weekend I drove with him to visit a number of small-town congregations around Arizona. He loved to teach children his philosophy of love."

There's nothing more life-affirming than death. When we are faced with mortality, people matter. Little things count. While honoring the departed, we find goodness in life. The vertical world opens up.

We see clouds crawl across the sky and hear whispers of angels in the trees. This window to the vertical world stays open for a few days, then it silently closes as we go about our business.

Don't let illness and death be your only reminders of the magnificence of life. Don't let your brain batter your soul with judgments and opinions. Practice beginner's mind. See opportunities. Experience the pleasures of this planet. Savor the beauty in every soul you meet.

Gently hold your attention in the present. Sure, you're bound to feel pain and disappointment. Yet if you relax, detach, center, then see like a poet, act like a child, and approach life with a beginner's mind, something new and intriguing will appear just around the corner.

"Ecstasy is what everyone craves," says Diane Ackerman, prize-winning poet, naturalist, and author of A *Natural History of the Senses*. "Not love or sex, but a hot-blooded, soaring intensity in which being alive is a joy and a thrill." Whether you want to glow with passion or be warmed by compassion, the present moment is the only "happening place" to be.

CHAPTER 9

Rapture at Work

Are you so busy
making a living
that you don't know
what you're living for?

—Twyman L. Towery

In his book *Flow: The Psychology of Optimal Experience*, Mihaly Csikszentmihalyi reports on a study that demonstrates an inner conflict many people have about what actually brings them happiness. To find out if people experience more instances of flow—a deep sense of enjoyment and freedom—at work or in times of leisure, Csikszentmihalyi surveyed more than 100 full-time workers. For one week, each wore an electronic pager that beeped randomly eight times a day. After every signal, the participants were to record what they were doing and how they were feeling.

Csikszentmihalyi found that participants felt strong, active, creative, and motivated for more than 50 percent of the time they spent at work. They recorded feelings of apathy, boredom, or frustration 16 percent of the time. In contrast, when engaged in leisure activities, the same respondents reported positive feelings only 18 percent of the time; most claimed they felt passive, weak, dull, and dissatisfied while not at work. "Even workers on the assembly lines reported they were in flow more than twice as often at work as in leisure, " Csikszentmihalyi writes.

The paradox is that when asked, "Where would you rather spend your time—on the job or away from it?" the great majority of people in our culture would either opt for the latter choice or say, "I would like to work less." Many admit to a desire to quit their jobs altogether if they win the lottery. No one wants to add hours to their workload.

Even the word *work* has negative connotations. It portrays jobs as "necessary evils" that divest us of time and enjoyment. As a result of this interpretation, we labor in a state of conditioned schizophrenia, continually sabotaging our capacity to find happiness on the job.

Why do we hold such a negative view of work? Why do we ignore the evidence our senses are giving us? Why is the experience of joy at work downplayed? It seems that if more people would acknowledge their good feelings on the job, workplaces would be much more pleasant.

OUR NEGATIVE VIEW OF WORK

Several factors erode the experience of happiness at work. One is the overriding sense of personal inadequacy evoked by the emphasis on status and material wealth. Our brains are obsessed with comparing our performance with that of our "more accomplished" peers. Further, with the worldwide penetration of television, job-related feelings of jealousy and inferiority have spread to cultures that for centuries took obvious delight in their work. Nearly everywhere, the motivation to work is now fueled by a perceived need for upscale clothes, expensive cars, and celebrity lifestyles.

The force of this mind-set hindered my attempts to teach leadership skills in Taiwan. Management, believing employees worked only for money, saw no reason to change their autocratic ways. Worse, supervisors and employees who worked for United States companies that paid more to their American counterparts were angrily locked into feeling cheated. Driven by the fear of never having enough income, they expended little energy on enhancing employee development and having fun.

As for business leaders in the West, many who have acquired status and material wealth are plagued by a crisis in self-respect. High-level managers and entrepreneurs alike confess to a fear of being "found out"; they worry that any wrong step they take will show they do not deserve their titles. The feeling of having "sold out," leaving behind their personal values in the climb to success, erodes their confidence even more. Happiness, they tell themselves, will come later, when they have enough money to retire. But "enough" is undefined. So they drive themselves senseless, working to the point of exhaustion, deadening their emotions, and estranging themselves from their families—a phenomenon that business researcher Mike Vandermark calls "joyless striving." It's no wonder that the highest occurrence of fatal heart attacks is on Monday mornings between 8:00 and 9:00, and that the stressor most often named by heart attack survivors is "job dissatisfaction."

According to Richard Sennett and Jonathan Cobb, coauthors of *The Hidden Injuries of Class,* a second factor that erodes the sense of joy in work settings is the perception of work as a loss of freedom. Where there is a boss, there is relinquishment of power. Any submanagement position is subject to contempt as well. For instance, although a janitor may own his home, drive a new car, and have money in the bank for his children's education, his subservient position exposes him to negative judgments from others. Worries about being loved, obtaining respect, and avoiding disdain often override his joy about receiving a regular paycheck.

Essentially, say Sennett and Cobb, any member of the workforce is entrenched in "the feeling of *not getting anywhere* despite one's efforts, the feeling of vulnerability in contrasting oneself to others at a higher social level, and the buried sense of inadequacy that one resents oneself for feeling." In addition to a pervasive sense of futility, fear of attack, and self-deprecation, there is an overriding belief that people at work don't care about one another. Coworkers are backstabbers, interested only in themselves. Trust is nonexistent.

As this negative view of work ripples down through the generations, the bitterness, frustration, and self-hatred magnify, suggesting that the American Dream has become more a burden than an inspiration. Worse, today's flood of books, audiotapes, infomercials, radio programs, television talk shows, sermons, and direct-mail campaigns that urge us to "follow your bliss" tends only to exacerbate the situation. People who subscribe to author Marsha Sinetar's advice to "do what you love, the money will follow" know what they want and have the financial reserves to build a business based on their passion. Others, however, feel doubly pressured to find their passion while lacking the security they believe is needed to search for it. These members of the workforce either hold fast to their bliss-hampering jobs, becoming increasingly miserable, or move from one job to another, finding flashes of satisfaction before succumbing again to loss of power and low self-esteem.

Our perception of work as an ogre that sucks us dry has become a mental virus of sorts. Richard Brodie, author of *Virus of the Mind*, defines these viruses as conspiracies of thought that spread with no conscious intent on our part. Nor can books about stress management or training programs in empowerment counteract their effects. Why? Because these viruses feed on beliefs. And beliefs, Brodie says, "are like cow paths. The more often you walk down a path, the more it looks like the right way to go." Even if it leads to the slaughterhouse, we might add.

Indeed, our disabling view of work is what festers at the core of today's epidemic of depression. To eradicate it, we must shatter the chains of the belief system that supports it. Ever so consciously, we must reprogram our minds to view work as an endeavor that promises happiness *while* affording us what we want for ourselves and our loved ones.

In the mid-nineteenth century, Scottish historian Thomas Carlyle said, "Blessed is he who has found his work." The most common interpretation is, "Blessed is he who has found work that suits his purpose." Yet Carlyle may actually have meant, "Blessed is he who has found his purpose *at* work." Instead of looking outside ourselves for dignity, fulfillment, and joy, we ought to be looking within, for that is where our happiness resides.

Rapture at work is a state of being, not doing. And being starts with the perception that joy can arise in *any* moment. When you feel joy at work, where you spend a good portion of your time, everything within you and around you benefits. As Csikszentmihalyi tells us, "If one finds flow in work...one is well on the way toward improving the quality of life as a whole."

CAN YOU LOVE YOUR WORK?

Actor George Burns, who led an active life until his death at age 100, said, "Imagine getting up every day hating what you have to do. That's what shortens your life." Actually, if you feel tired, frustrated, angry, bored, or distracted for hours each day at work, every segment of your life suffers—your relationships, your ability to see opportunities, your health and peace of mind, and your capacity to relax. Interestingly, words you use to describe your work may be the same ones you use to summarize your life. If work is a drag, chances are that your life is unstimulating, as well.

To evaluate your current level of job dissatisfaction, complete the questionnaire shown in figure 9–1. Acknowledge yourself for your 4's and 5's. To increase your happiness at work, shift your attitude in the areas marked by 1's and 2's.

Figure 9–1

How Dissatisfied Am I?

For each statement, circle the number, from 1 to 5, that best represents your impressions at work. Then add up your score.

		Strongly agree				Strongly disagree
1.	I am the only one who can do my job.	1	2	3	4	5
2.	Everything must be done the "right" way.	1	2	3	4	5
3.	I don't settle for less than perfection.	1	2	3	4	5
4.	When I'm less than perfect, I'm deficient.	1	2	3	4	5
5.	I'm often bored, confused, or anxious.	1	2	3	4	5
6.	I often feel guilty or angry.	1	2	3	4	5
7.	I dread going to work.	1	2	3	4	5
8.	I frequently compare my work with that of others.	1	2	3	4	5
9.	I never seek help from others.	1	2	3	4	5
10.	My mind drifts from one task to another.	1	2	3	4	5

	Strongly agree				Strongly disagree
11. I reflect on my mistakes for a long time.	1	2	3	4	5
12. I often focus on what might go wrong.	1	2	3	4	5
13. My coworkers waste time and don't think.	1	2	3	4	5
14. I avoid making friends at work.	1	2	3	4	5
15. I hate looking or sounding stupid.	1	2	3	4	5
16. I take a day off only when I'm sick in bed.	1	2	3	4	5
17. I'll catch up someday.	1	2	3	4	5
18. People talk about me behind my back.	1	2	3	4	5
19. When all else fails, I try harder.	1	2	3	4	5
20. I never get to choose what to do.	1	2	3	4	5
21. Meaningful work is an oxymoron.	1	2	3	4	5
22. I never get the appreciation I deserve.	1	2	3	4	5
23. I work harder than everyone else.	1	2	3	4	5
24. There is no way to improve my situation.	1	2	3	4	5
25. I cannot feel free in my current job.	1	2	3	4	5
Totals	+	+	+	+	=

A score of less than 50 suggests that you may be prone to depression, exhaustion, and physical illness. To reverse the debilitating effects of work, practice the techniques described in the remainder of this chapter. Also consider seeking the help of a therapist or coach to overcome perceptual blocks and generate a more positive frame of mind.

If your score is between 50 and 95, you probably go home feeling tired and powerless. To regain energy, consider what it will take to raise your 3's to 4's or 5's. Work on these items one at a time. Then concentrate on raising your 2's, and finally your 1's. Strive to reach a score of at least 100.

If your score is over 95, congratulations! You've succeeded in overcoming the impact of cultural norms. To further enhance your joy at work, examine each statement for which you scored a 1 or a 2, and ask yourself if an unmet need is at play here. If it is, either satisfy the need, downgrade it, or make peace with yourself by letting it go.

Whatever your score is, you can no doubt enjoy work more than you currently do, and radiate more joy as well. For starters, consider shifting your perspective of work from a labor of pain to a labor of love. As Lebanese poet Kahlil Gibran said, "To live life through labor is to be intimate with life's inmost secret. All work is empty save when there is love, for work is love made visible." The key is not to change *what you do,* but to change *who you are* in relation to your tasks. You can see yourself as a laborer or a master, a sacrificer or an artist, a slave or a contributor, a peon or a prodigy. The image you hold of yourself at work determines how you feel about your job.

Researchers have found that self-image also affects capability. Scores of studies show that children either excel or fail based on the labels their parents and teachers assigned to them. Similarly, the extent to which you excel is determined by the limits you create in your mind, which may cause you to quit long before you reach your potential. Extend or vanish these limits and you just might soar—a possibility too often overlooked. As psychologist Abraham Maslow said, "The unhappiness, unease and unrest in the world today are caused by people living far below their capacity."

So what inspires us to view ourselves as vital, reach for our potential, and enjoy ourselves in the process? Novelist James Michener unraveled this puzzle eloquently when he wrote: "The master in the art of living makes little distinction between his work and his play, his labor and his leisure.... He hardly knows which is which. He simply pursues his vision of excellence at whatever he does, leaving others to decide whether he is working or playing. To him, he's always doing both." The answer, it seems, is to transition from a full-time job to a full-time life in which work and play form a seamless flow of being.

To help catalyze this transition for yourself, recognize that at any point in time you're feeling exactly what you *choose* to feel. You therefore have no business blaming your emotions on your coworkers, your boss, or your stack of unpaid bills. You can choose to feel as if you've surrendered your soul in return for a paycheck. Or you can choose to shift into a more positive state. You can choose to be angry or choose to be peaceful. You can choose to worry or choose to be playful. You can choose to be busy or choose to masterfully compose.

Richard Barrett, who teaches spirituality in the workplace, chose to find passion on the job. Throughout his thirty-year work life, he had been successful at everything he tackled. Yet every new venture seemed to entail seeking and suffering, succeeding and fleeing, prosperity and unhappiness. When his values began to shift from amassing money and titles to discovering meaningful work, few people supported his transition. Making your work a work of art is not for the timid of heart, Barrett tells us. When everyone around you behaves just the opposite, you must courageously stand up for your beliefs. "It requires personal struggle," he adds. "Only when you change internally will you see those benefits reflected in the outside world. You have to go through a process, and it's painful. You have to show up fearlessly"—like a hero.

As daunting as it may be, there's nothing more liberating than bringing your body, mind, and heart with you to work. When you connect what you do with what you most value, a huge weight is lifted. Your neck and shoulders loosen up. Your smile comes out to play. Your spirit is awakened and free to fly.

Are you willing to take on the challenge? If so, begin by ensuring that your work is pleasurable, even energizing. And quit expecting others to alter your impressions for you. You alone are responsible for these pictures. Historian Edward Gibbon noted, "When the Athenians finally wanted not to give to society but for society to give to them, when the freedom they wished for was the freedom from responsibility, then Athens ceased to be free." You make the choices. Therein lies your freedom, and your potential for rapture at work.

REALIGNING YOUR BEHAVIOR AT WORK

Acknowledging that you can indeed love your work will strengthen your foundation while you're there. Now it's time to actually love the work, and to keep that love alive. This mission requires certain behavioral adjustments, to ensure that your actions will assist you in achieving your purpose.

Start by taking your personal power inventory (see pages 32–33) with you to work. Then, any time you anticipate a difficult situation, review the list to remind yourself of your greatest strengths. Remember, you were hired for these virtues. Your skills are an asset. Your ideas are valuable. As you walk down the hall, be your powers.

Second, inventory your beliefs about work. Do you believe work can be fun and meaningful? Do you think you're able to improve your attitude? Do you think others can help you? If you've answered "no" to these questions, is there a chance you might be wrong and that today you'll see the light? Optimism is the primary ingredient of happiness at work.

Third, review your top ten fears to see if any of them are intruding into your day. Do you feel inadequate in comparison with others? Are you holding back insights for fear of being laughed at or hurting someone else's feelings? Identify the fears that keep you from being magnificent. Then eradicate the lies they are rooted in (see page 37), replacing them with positive beliefs.

Integrate these statements into your daily existence: *I am not stupid. I deserve success. I can solve problems. It's okay to ask for more time and training. I am a good person and need not take responsibility for what others think. I am significant. Work can be a joyful experience.* If you have a hard time embodying any of these statements, repeat the unconvincing ones several times a day for a few weeks. Feel them in your heart as you say them. Act *as if* you believe them and soon you will. If you need help, ask a colleague who is interested in personal growth to team up with you. Periodically remind each other of the belief you're trying to incorporate. Be there for each other when you need to talk, or set up mutually convenient times to meet. Having a buddy to call on as you work through a fear is invaluable. Spend time with people who support you. Limit your time with folks who bring you down.

Fourth, for additional support in realigning your behavior at work, review your needs list (see page 98), especially when you're feeling angry, rebellious, vengeful, frustrated, apathetic, resigned, or anxious. Digging below the surface for the cause of your reaction, identify the unmet need. Here are some clues:

- A need for *approval* or *acceptance* will cause you to hide behind routines, refusing to take risks, overcommitting to tasks, and doing other people's work. Looking closely, you will see that your actions are designed to either ward off criticism or attract positive attention. Unmet, these needs can lead to a restrained rage, stripping you of vitality.

- A need for *acknowledgment, appreciation, love,* or *respect* will drive you not only to overwork but to demand perfection of your work. You may be hypersensitive to criticism, victimized by self-doubt, and constantly judging your work performance against that of others. The need to *be important* may cause you to react in similar ways.

- A need for *prosperity* will have you overpowered by a desire to make money, have possessions, and see immediate results. The need for *achievement* sparks comparable desires.

- The need to *control* will have you doing everything possible to avoid being seen as vulnerable, weak, worthless, stupid, or incompetent. The thought of letting anyone see your all-too-human flaws is unbearable when this need stages a revolt. The need to *be right* and the need to *win* stir up similar reactions.

- The need for *harmony*, on the other hand, will keep you from standing up for yourself when you are right or when you should take charge of a situation. Wounds fester and problems multiply while you busily try to smooth things over.

- The need for *consistency* will stunt your growth. You'll become lost in complaining about change, no matter how inevitable or beneficial it may be. Eventually, you'll be left behind.

Need-based behaviors often take the fun out of work, paralyzing our passion and injuring our relationships. Needs can have a positive effect as well, helping us achieve desired results. Control is often useful while managing a project. Harmony can elicit a promotion. Consistency keeps daily tasks on track. The key is to identify when your actions are driven by a need, and then determine if continuing these actions is beneficial or detrimental. Remember, control your needs or they will control you.

To decide whether to meet your need or let it go, ask yourself, "Is this need serving me or draining me?" If it is serving you, ask, "Is it really important to satisfy this need?" Be honest. If meeting the need will result in positive outcomes, go for it. If not, detach from the need's hold on you, using the technique described in figure 9–2.

Successful need management also requires on-site follow-through.

FIGURE 9–2

Detaching from a Need

The sooner you detach from a need that depletes your energy or lacks importance in attaining your desired results, the sooner you will return to a state of emotional balance at work. For assistance, complete these steps.

- Any time you feel a strong negative emotion, look for the need that is governing your thoughts.

- When you find the need, visualize it as a gremlin screaming in your brain. Mentally, grab the gremlin and remove it from your head, setting it on a corner of your desk. Talk to the gremlin with firm conviction, explaining that you're in charge. Then decide whether or not to meet the need.

- If more than one need is acting out, seat them around a table. Tell them that you are the wise and noble King Arthur, and that you are about to operate on behalf of the highest good. Then decide which of these needs, if any, you will meet. Ask the others to go in peace, explaining that although they are a part of you, they are not currently serving your best interests. Feel the release in your heart.

If after detaching from a need you decide to change your behavior or a procedure, let your coworkers know why you've made this decision. Aware of your motives, they will be more apt to go with your flow. Modeling self-awareness as well as self-control is a sign of leadership.

Also, remember to keep up your self-care. Happiness is resistant to sleep deprivation, poor nutrition, noise pollution, excessive conflict, lack of money, and a shortage of friends. Your mental house must be clean for joy to enter.

RESTRUCTURING YOUR PERCEPTION OF WORK

How you view work is as vital as how you behave there. In fact, in restructuring your perception of work you reinvent your workplace. This feat hinges on two factors: discovery and visioning. First, you discover the "soul values" of the job you are performing. Then you vision effective ways to capitalize on these values. The picture you compose will guide you through your day-to-day business.

Discovery

Many clients who come to me for coaching are frustrated with their work and disappointed with their lives. Invariably, they are most disturbed by their perception of having accomplished nothing of major significance. When they started their careers, they had either visions of fame or plans for moving up the career ladder fast enough to retire early with grace and a small fortune. Twenty years later, they're still muddling away, staring at another twenty years of thankless toil.

After learning to be fully present at work and to approach it with a beginner's mind, they are able to peer into the looking glass of their souls—an odyssey you, too, can embark on by practicing the exercise described in figure 9–3. As psychologist Ron Browning says, "It is in the mundane that we must first learn to recognize the spiritual."

Paul, a client of mine, found that it often takes a child's perspective to see the soul values of work. Long embarrassed by his father, who worked on a road crew, Paul did a turnabout after hearing his eight-year-old son describe the job in glowing terms. "Granddad drove these great big machines that took years to learn how to handle," his son said. "And he had to operate the controls just right. Plus, he used a walkie-talkie to stay in touch with the guys driving other machines.

Figure 9–3

Discover Your Soul Values

The beauty you find in job-related activities tells you what's important to your soul. Once you have this information, work transforms into an art you can take pleasure in mastering. Insignificant details become profound, and frustrations lighten into either humorous incidents or labors of love. To uncover the beauty in your job, take time to reflect on your answers to these questions.

- What aspects of your job do you enjoy? Do you like to work on the computer, or read articles on the latest research in your field of interest? Maybe you prefer to write, or analyze problems on paper. Is crunching numbers more a game than a chore? Which mode of working do you like best—figuring out ways to increase efficiency on your own, helping newer employees excel, or networking with colleagues?

- How are you of service to your customers? What brings you the most pleasure when you interact with them? What compliments do you most like to hear about your-self and your work?

- When do you feel positively challenged? On hectic days, do you enjoy stretching your skills and increasing your wisdom?

- Under what circumstances do you feel most secure—when you have a reserve of money or when you find meaning, learn lessons, and partner with others?

- What little details at your workplace bring on a smile? Are you grateful for the warm cup of coffee someone handed you last week, the funny cartoon that was left on your desk yesterday, or perhaps the security guard who raved about your new car?

And he had his own radio to sing along with all day. When he was done, people had a safe road to drive on. That's cool."

Whether you find your soul values by using the eyes of a poet or those of a child, your future at work will be forever changed. Why? Because after discovering the joy in what you do for a living, you *never have to "work" another day in your life*. In the course of doing your tasks, you get to be anything your soul desires. While answering the phone or writing a progress report, identify the details that inspire you to feel compassionate, playful, and respectful—or whatever traits your soul most values. When do you feel excited, secure, and proud? When could you feel happier, more satisfied, and grateful? Hold the positive aspects up to the light. Your work life will shine more brightly.

Keep your mind open to these possibilities during your commute to and from work as well. While driving, see the road as an amusement ride instead of a racetrack. Instead of cutting through traffic to gain five minutes of time—and stress-related damage to your heart—use the five minutes for centering. Listen to the radio or a tape. Notice the scenery. Observe the faces of your fellow drivers as they wait impatiently for the red light to turn green. Did you ever notice that no matter how fast they take off down the street, there they are waiting impatiently at the next red light? Cultivate your sense of humor by seeing the funny side of life.

Joy on the job rarely comes in a flash of enlightenment. Most often, it unfolds with diligent practice. A commitment to discovering sources of joy is often required to counteract the brainwashing that convinced us work is a drag. So practice discovering every day. Eventually, your frustrations and disappointments will melt away.

Visioning
Through visioning what is possible, you integrate your job with your life. When the integration is complete, how you earn a living will mesh with who you see yourself being at your best.

To prepare, review the vision you created while reading chapter 5. Whether you wrote a narrative, drew a picture, or cut up magazines, study the images you composed to represent who you are while fully alive. Recall the feelings you experienced at the time, bringing them into the present moment. Then, using the exercise described in figure 9–4, add job-related details to your vision.

FIGURE 9–4

Your Ideal Day at Work

To weave your workday into your vision of who you are, follow these guidelines.

- Sit back and imagine a perfect day at work one year from now. Include the entire spectrum of sensory experiences— what you see, hear, touch, taste, and smell. Focus fully on who you are being.

- Now concentrate on what you are doing and how you are bringing your "self" to work. Visualize your best self interacting with your manager, peers, employees, and customers. Then see yourself doing more tasks you take pleasure in and fewer jobs you find distasteful. Identify your most valuable contributions to the workplace.

- Picture yourself engaging in self-care measures—taking breaks to restore your energy and perspective, going for walks, stretching your body, and eating healthful snacks.

- Once you have a clear picture of your perfect day at work, initiate actions that can take you there.

To stay on track, keep your vision alive. Set aside daily "think tank" time, when your mind is not racing, to review your vision, reset priorities, detach from conflicts and gossip, determine the problems you want to take responsibility for, and commit to your choices. If possible, redesign your work space to conform with your vision. Move your chair and desk. Arrange for a more convenient filing system. Perhaps work with feng shui principles, or consult with a designer who specializes in bringing balance and harmony to the workplace.

Evolving from who you are now to who you envision may require the full twelve months. And well it should—since shifts in procedures, relationships, environment, and most of all perception are often gradual. At some point, you may begin to see your workplace with new eyes, coming to peace with your job and deriving pleasure from the tasks it entails.

On the other hand, you may find your present circumstances too dysfunctional to help you achieve your vision. Perhaps a different workplace would be more suitable, or maybe you are ready to leap fully into another occupation. In either event, be sure to imagine a nourishing environment in which the dispensation of your gifts brings you prosperity. To round out the picture, link up with people who have made winning leaps. Then, before jumping, check out the terrain at the bottom of the cliff—or better yet, learn what it will take to lay it out with a bed of feathers by planning for contingencies and ensuring that you have a reserve of time, friends, energy, and money to get you through the transition. Finally, see yourself as a successful risk-taker.

Whether or not you decide to change your workplace or your occupation, integrating your work into the manifestation of who you are promises rich dividends. As you pursue your passion, a job you don't like or tasks you don't care for become secondary, and no longer a source of exhaustion. When you know that your workday is carrying you one step closer to living your vision, job-related fears and resentments decrease. These outcomes arise not because you've numbed yourself to your work or dissociated from it, but because you've embraced it. No longer are you working; instead, you are *creating*.

QUIT GOING TO WORK

The factor that most stifles joy in the workplace is our negative view of work as laborious, difficult, and tedious. Corporate cultures that encourage complaining and distrust augment this perception. Mired in these invalidating images, we are unable to acknowledge how strong, active, imaginative, positively challenged, and motivated we feel while laboring eight or more hours a day at our jobs.

The solution? It's time to quit going to work. When you leave home in the morning, see yourself as going off to *create*. Instead of asking people what they do for work, ask them what type of creating they do.

Transforming your own perceptions in this regard is one thing. Transforming your colleagues' perceptions, in an effort to reinvent your workplace, is quite another. Depending on the degree of negativity that exists, you may at first be seen as a clown or a scapegoat. Nobody likes a smiling face when they're intent on being unhappy. What do you do? You withstand the derision. For your own peace of mind—and ultimately your coworkers' as well—your commitment to improving the climate must be unflappable.

What's next? Follow Gandhi's advice to "be the change you want to make in the world." In other words, go straight to being. Be the person you see in your vision. While solving complex problems, acknowledge the fun you're having instead of wallowing in the frustration. Take on challenges with excitement, not resentment. Accept and build on others' ideas, rather than finding fault with them. Let your light shine. Others will follow.

This endeavor requires *persistence*. Believe that transformation is possible. See your colleagues as capable achievers who want to be acknowledged for their work and their wisdom. Also see them as people driven by fears of being belittled, bullied, and compared negatively with others. Show compassion, fairness, and respect. Your colleagues are apt to respond in kind.

If there's a coworker you don't like, practice beginner's mind. Commit to finding within the person an attribute you admire. Listen for knowledge they may have on a topic you know little about. Psychiatrist Howard Cutler recommends a related approach—softening your judgment. Do you hate the person's hair (fingernails, hands, eyes)? Find a trait you *don't* dislike, and focus on that. Model the tolerance you want to see. Change will follow.

Although most people in our culture regard the workplace as the last bastion to welcome merriment and joy, that is precisely what is needed to maintain a healthy economy. Only individuals who feel passion for their work can tap into their potential. So help to break down the wall that separates work from play. Go about your day as if rapture might erupt at any moment. Find satisfaction, pleasure, and significance in your responsibilities. Recognize that you are serving your purpose.

If you show up committed to your vision, the rewards will be sweet. You will be paid for being happy. Your happiness will be infectious. You may even be held accountable for spreading an epidemic of joy.

CHAPTER 10

Rapture at Play

I have longed to give voice to the child within me.
With her voice, I can step boldly
through the doors marked "no" and
reclaim my passion for living.

—Bonnie Henry

The real tragedy inherent in today's society is not our attitude about work, but the waste of what we call our "free" or "leisure" time. When we're not at work, we're presumably at play. But how playful do we allow ourselves to be?

Most people, when asked how they feel during their time off, reply, "Fine." Often, this stock response seems an acronym for "feelings inaccessible—near empty." Certainly, many of us spend our free time feeling apathetic, bored, and unfulfilled—in short, lifeless.

What a sorry state of affairs we've constructed in forgetting how to play. During the week, the interlude between leaving the workplace and returning to it is far from memorable. Weekends are no better: we spend them completing to-do lists or pumping up our adrenaline by watching others compete. Then we seek out the company of strangers to share in chemically induced laughter.

Rarely do we stretch our comfort zones by indulging in naturally induced fun—at least not for extended periods of time. Some people who catch themselves acting nonsensically quickly apologize for their momentary display of "childish" spontaneity. We adults, it seems, have not only forgotten how to play but have become ashamed of our playful instincts.

Worse, there is little freedom in our "free time." We program ourselves to race around while vacationing and to judge unplanned situations as annoyances. We sacrifice happiness for our families and lovers. We forfeit joy to reach goals. We stifle laughter and tears in the name of "maturity." Highly developed in the art of not feeling, we've locked the door to our emotions. Although we may cry over a sad movie or the loss of a friend, we immediately rein in our emotions and send them back to confinement. Eventually, some of our harnessed emotions, such as sadness and anger, erupt when least expected. Others, such as love, die from starvation.

Our emotional inertia is terminal. After shutting down our hearts at work, we drag our exhausted, disheartened hulls home to vegetate, medicate, and entertain with electronic toys until it's time to return to work. According to cardiologist and psychotherapist Stephen Sinatra, MD, in his book *Optimum Health*, "Just as stagnant water can become toxic, the blocking of [our] feelings, intuition, pleasures, and desires can be equally toxic." The result is not only frustration and unhappiness, but also stress, illness—often heart disease—and ultimately, death.

Clearly, what you do in your leisure time is far less important than how you feel while doing it. Do you feel lighthearted, curious, and excited, perhaps passionate? When you finish, do you feel inwardly warm and rejuvenated? Whether dancing, singing, running, playing the guitar, driving your car, organizing your closet, brushing your daughter's hair, talking with your father, skydiving, or sky watching, do you come away feeling alive? Actually, you can be playful doing *anything*. Why? Because playfulness is a state of "being." As soon as you become present to who you are in the moment, you can capture the rapturous sense of play.

While in this state of mind, you can see that life is meant to be random, downright messy at times, juicy, rowdy, goofy, loud, chaotic, sensual, and yummy. Charlotte Kasl, PhD, writes, in *If the Buddha Dated*, "When you're alive, that's what you're supposed to be doing—being alive." Kids don't wait for a day off to have fun, and they don't volunteer to do their chores before playing. Nor do they *plan* to make food sculptures. They do what they feel like doing—and so can you. I'm not suggesting that you dump sand on the carpet. But you might try finger painting or slapping your feet in a puddle if your soul moves you to do so. Regardless of the activity you choose, if you breathe, check in, and follow your feelings, you'll know what it means to embrace life.

How do you know what your soul wants you to do? By disencumbering your mind and clearing the channel to your heart. There you will find your soul's desires.

UNBURDENING YOUR MIND

We are weighed down mightily by our particular bundle of needs. Those that most commonly curb spontaneity are the need for safety, the need to be liked, and the need to achieve—all of which lure us away from dallying on the path of the present moment. Other needs also play a role, especially those that magnetize us to the TV or computer screen, miles from the dance floor. If I could take back all the moments I've lost to worrying about how people were judging me, obsessing over my ability to succeed, and debating over whether I'd made the right decision long after arriving at it, I'd probably double my life span. Now I'm learning to quit trying so hard. For me, *freedom* is another word for "nothing left to need."

To unburden your own mind, take stock of the gremlins that are lurking there. Dig deep to catch the little ones that keep you from carving a face in the peanut butter, from thoughtfully arranging flowers in a vase, or from sending a limerick to friends you haven't seen in a while, ending the note with how much you miss their company.

Confer with the gremlins you find, and let them know you're taking back your playtime. That night—as well as the next one, and the following weekend—set out for the "playground of life" intent on having fun. For maximum enjoyment, abide by these eight rules.

Figure 10–1

Playground Rules

1. No running.
Life is blurry in the fast lane. To inch your way out of it, teach yourself to slowly take in your surroundings. This practice will boost your happiness far more than clearing your to-do list in record time. You'll finish the chores. It just might take longer.

2. Turn off the TV and sign off the Internet.
Instead, plug into curiosity. What shape is tonight's moon? Has anyone on your block planted a new cluster of flowers? How is your best friend feeling? What does your lover's skin feel like from her wrist to her elbow, or from his lips to his eyes? Can you devise a new recipe for brownies, name the species of birds in your yard, make up a game to play with your children? Shake yourself up and come alive.

3. Stop whining.
Complaints bear down heavily on human wings. To shed your propensity for whining, set an alarm to go off every two hours whether you're at home, the grocery store, or the golf course. Each time it goes off, write down what you're doing and how you're feeling. At the end of the day, review your notes. Are you happy with how you spent your free time? If not, can you alter your schedule, or your perceptions of it? If nothing else, streamline your unenjoyable tasks or pay someone to do them. Enter the playground ready for delight and the whining will evaporate.

4. Choose your playmates well.
Dour playmates cast dreary shadows. Keep the playground atmosphere bright by bringing along cheerful friends—people you can laugh, daydream, imagine, conjecture, and be silly with.

5. Let go of your ego.

Laugh at your mistakes. Celebrate your flimsy faults—the harmless parts of you that are less than ideal yet all too human. When you feel sad in response to someone's actions, let them know; then find something capricious to do together. Admit to being embarrassed; then squirt a shaving-cream caricature of your face on the bathroom mirror. Deflate your need for perfection or importance. Before long, you'll feel lighter than air.

6. Don't worry, be happy.

If years of working in the corporate world have taught you never to touch another person, risk a neutral yet caring physical connection. Squeeze someone's shoulder, clasp hands, pat a back. Also, touch, hug, and kiss dear friends whenever you can. Your soul will smile, and so will theirs.

7. Wear play clothes.

Dress for comfort. Wear loose-fitting clothes that you can safely bend in, wrinkle, and dirty. The message to send through your choice in clothing is: I'm here to relax and have a good time.

8. Experiment and explore.

Try new activities, and approach tried-and-true ones in new ways. Change your routines. Take different roads to familiar destinations. Try out a new musical instrument. Deliver homegrown flowers to a cranky neighbor. Throw a tomato as far as you can. Eat ice cream for breakfast and oatmeal with raisins and cinnamon for dinner. Converse with fellow passengers in an elevator. Compliment the receptionist at the doctor's office. Sing out loud before falling asleep. Jump out of bed when you wake up. Keep experimenting and the present will be too much fun to leave.

BREAKING THROUGH TO JOY

Are you ready to let down your guard and truly play? If so, switch your awareness meter to "on," declare your independence from greedy needs, spread your wings, and fly. It doesn't take more time, more money, better friends, or a smoother marriage to find joy in washing the car, for instance. Write your name in soap, splash water over it, and shine the chrome till you can see your reflection in it. If you're part-way through and not having fun, then pay ten dollars to have the car washed while you read humorous greeting cards in the waiting area. As you do, be sure to laugh out loud.

Any leisure-time activity can spark happiness provided that you remain conscious of your sensory experiences and stop the task when it's no longer fun. Pleasure can bubble up while you work on your monthly budget or write a letter to the editor of your local paper—even while you set the table or sort the laundry. Any experience can give rise to rapture; you just need to clear the way to it.

Happiness erupts each time your soul expresses itself. In such moments, you may feel God speaking through you or a creative life force flowing through you. This free flow of energy—unobstructed by the voices in your head—can produce great art, whether you're writing, painting, drafting an architectural blueprint, or arranging vegetables on a platter. And the freedom itself is delicious.

If happiness does not erupt spontaneously, practice beginner's mind. Look at every circumstance, event, and person, including yourself, as if seeing it for the first time. Then uncover a fascinating aspect about it. In diverting your attention from a physical pain or a less-than-magnificent week to a source of wonder, you'll enter the realm of the possible, where boredom and misery evaporate.

For another direct path to happiness, cancel the "when-then" tape in your head that advises, "When this happens, then I'll _____." Either pursue your dream now or find joy in a current situation. My friend Kate, who stuck with the tape, agreed to go out with me only after losing twenty pounds. She is still sitting around feeling sorry for herself.

Also destroy the "I'm too old to _____" tape. Many people in their sixties trek Nepal and take up windsurfing.

The best way to discover what brings you joy is by practicing awareness every day. Wake up your senses. See, hear, smell, touch, and taste with vigor. Life is a buffet. Taste a little of everything.

To prepare for days when obligations dampen your mood, put together a jar full of joy, following the directions given in figure 10–2.

A variation on this technique, outlined in figure 10–3, will help while you're away from home. Smiling, you'll find, is the quickest way through the ice of monotony, aggravation, and discontent. Replace with a grin the voluntary reactions of numbness, contempt, and gloom and you'll be able to choose from an array of different emotions. If you begin to wonder whether or not playing is "appropriate," acknowledge this voice and ask it to leave. Feel your fear or embarrassment, and proceed anyway. Embracing the moment is better than later regretting its loss.

FIGURE 10–2

A Jar Full of Joy

To offset leisure-time lows with refreshing highs, follow these instructions. Preparation time is minimal, and gratification immediate.

- On two sheets of paper, front only, list at least fifty activities that make you smile. State each one as an instruction, giving it a line of its own, and omit any activity that calls for planning or for more than 1 hour of travel.

    My list includes the following: paint pottery; color a picture outside of the lines; drive to the summit of South Mountain, then stand on the hood of the car and belt out a show tune; look for animal shapes in the clouds; play with a talking stuffed animal; take my neighbor's dog for a run; lie on the floor petting my cat; sing along with a Jana Stanfield or Janis Joplin CD; dance like a ghoul to Camille Saint-Säens's *Danse Macabre*; four-wheel in the Ford Explorer; stretch out in cool grass beneath a tree; play with my godson; make love; write a love poem; sprawl on the floor head-to-head with a girlfriend and talk about everything under the sun; clean my desk; remove clutter from the closet and garage; send a fun greeting card to a friend for no reason; get a foot massage; slip into a freshly made bed for a midday nap; leisurely apply make-up; daydream on the couch while listening to soft music; visit the zoo or a wildlife preserve; pet cats at the no-kill shelter; stretch; and take a bubble bath.

- Cut out each instruction, producing strips of paper that look like this:

> Get a foot massage

Fold up each strip and drop it into a jar. You now have a jar full of joy.

- Place the filled jar in an easy-to-reach spot. Then any time you're home and have not smiled for two hours, choose a strip of paper and follow the instructions. If for any reason you cannot pursue this activity, because of the weather or the time of day or the mood you're in, choose another strip. The point is to do something that opens your heart.

FIGURE 10–3

A Pocket of Joy

To balance out sour moods while traveling, prepare this portable rendition of your jar full of joy. Think of it as your smiles-to-go emergency kit.

- On a sheet of paper, list at least ten activities that are sure to prompt a smile while you're on the road. Consider these activities: call someone to tell them you love them; get a shoe shine; find a fresh flower for your room away from home; drink a milk shake; walk down a street you've never seen; stretch every muscle in your body; buy a pocket toy; smile seductively at yourself in a mirror; smile seductively at a stranger; get a pedicure; draw a cartoon of someone who irritates you; take in the savory aroma of local spices.

- Cut out each item; fold it; and drop it into a small envelope.

- While preparing for a trip, stuff the envelope in your pocket or purse. For best results, never leave home without it.

Once you've discovered how to be happy at play, begin to incorporate these forms of upliftment into your everyday life—before work, after work, and on weekends. Let joy be a ribbon that weaves through work and play, binding them together.

To urge you on, rally together a support group of family and friends who champion your commitment to happiness—or at the very least, who acknowledge your dedication to personal development. Remember, you are not the only one to benefit. Seeing the glow you emanate, others are sure to want some radiance for themselves.

Playing—living life spontaneously—demonstrates to others that you believe in the soul's existence. Although it may feel uncomfortable at first, basking in the rapture of the moment is the height of self-actualization. Know that laughter, rather than obstructing productivity, will increase creativity. Levity, rather than harming relationships, will deepen the bonds that secure them. Playfulness, rather than minimizing accountability, will lighten your surroundings with the effervescence of celebration. If we all had permission to be who we really are, love would finally overpower fear.

The challenge, then, is to feel. Let your child out to play. And if on this quest you encounter sorrow, shame, grief, terror, frustration, rage, embarrassment, or nervous excitement, then say hello to the emotions that make you uniquely you. Talk about them, cry, scream, laugh uncontrollably, and stomp around the room. As the energy is released, relish in your freedom. Very soon, you will not only remember how to play but also reclaim your passion for living.

CHAPTER 11

Rapture in Relationships

*It's not the seven-dollar beer
that makes life good—
it's the people you're drinking it with.*

—Wendy Reid Crisp

While waiting for a massage, I recounted the indignity my boyfriend caused me when he chose to go to sleep early rather than take me out the night before. Don listened as he set up the massage table. After a few minutes of whining, I apologized and said, "If this is my biggest worry, I should be grateful rather than bitch about staying home alone one Saturday night."

Don replied, casually, "There is nothing shameful about your disappointment. Most people spend their lives in survival mode—making money for food and shelter, and protecting themselves from harm. You, on the other hand, have taken care of these matters. They no longer consume you. Instead, you're busy defining yourself in relationship to others. You're learning how to open yourself to love, which is the ultimate experience. When we've reached the point of wanting nothing but love, we truly know the honor of being human."

He smoothed out the wrinkles on the top sheet. "Ready?" he asked. "I'll go wash my hands."

I was stunned, my mind blown away by Don's wisdom. Was love really the ultimate life experience? If so, everything I professed to know about self-actualization, self-sufficiency, and self-love was on trial. If loving relationships were essential to joy, I would have to reconcile my campaign, maybe even my life's purpose, with this notion.

Aware that God works in mysterious ways, I was not surprised to receive a call three days later from my best friend Debbie, whom I'd known for thirty-eight years. She told me about a mutual friend's illness, and we made plans to visit her. After hanging up, I called my friend of eighteen years, Paul, to reschedule dinner. I went on to tell him about the business meeting I had the day before, and how lucky I felt to have such good rapport with my clients. I also told him I'd spent the previous afternoon with my niece, laughing at old pictures and reading my father's love poems as we ransacked my back bedroom closet in search of clues to help her construct a family tree. Paul then invited me to dinner Friday night so that I could meet his current flame. I told him I'd be delighted, and proceeded to recount my latest dating adventure.

Don was right, I told myself after saying goodbye. Our relationships form the glue that holds together the fabric of our being. No matter what we accomplish in terms of personal achievement, the happiness we feel depends on the intensity of the love we share with others.

Pushing through a variety of fears, I resolved to open my heart fully—to my lover, colleagues, friends, and enemies. And each time I did, barriers crumbled. I saw that I could be openly honest about *all* my feelings and survive, even be liked. I acknowledged the joy my present relationships brought me and the cherished memories I'd been given by my family, friends, and lovers. I could also allow myself to fully feel the pain of disappointment and the sorrow from loss. In fact, releasing this flow of heart energy increased the peacefulness in my life. No longer worried about what was okay to say or do, I could stay in the moment. Better yet, my emotional candor often freed the *other* person to open *their* heart. When this happened, a sacred bond formed between us. For a moment, our souls shook hands, confirming all that was holy within us.

The Latin translation for being alive means, literally, "being among men." Certainly, babies deprived of touch don't grow. People who live alone have the highest incidence of illness and depression. Shunning and isolation are used as extreme forms of punishment worldwide. And people with rock-solid confidence feel devastated when hurt by their "true love."

The joy we feel while receiving love has been likened to knowing God. It instills us with energy and a sense of significance. Devoid of human connections, we become exhausted, congested, cut off from our moorings. In the words of *Optimal Health* author Stephen Sinatra, PhD, "The denial of love, denial of human contact, and denial of emotional outlets clog the system just as surely as do fats and cholesterol." Without the bonding of flesh and spirit, one window stays closed, suffocating the soul.

Opening that window, we savor life by tasting the sweetness, spiciness, and bitterness of intimacy. In loving others, we activate passion. In feeling loved, we experience joy.

So which comes first—self-love or loving others? Before my encounter with Don, I was convinced we cannot love another until we love ourselves. Now, I believe the journey to love can proceed on two parallel yet interdependent paths. When we progress along one— learning either how to love ourselves or how to love others—we move forward on both. In essence, as you free yourself of fears and needs, you become better able to embrace the pleasure of a shared moment. And as you open yourself to loving others, you gain a greater understanding and acceptance of yourself.

It's true that you must love at least parts of yourself in order to love another. Yet the converse is also true: knowing that you are loved enables you to embrace the other parts of yourself. Once you recognize that someone loves you—despite your fat, wrinkles, phobias, and frailties—you cannot help but move toward fully loving yourself.

Self-actualization, like self-love, does not manifest in a vacuum. To think you can realize your potential without the help of others is an illusion. While trying to figure out your latent capacities, you need someone to talk to, someone to listen, even someone to disagree with your rambling thoughts. Yet the paths, while dependent, must stay parallel. For a fruitful quest, neither learning how to love yourself nor learning how to love others can dominate.

THE TRUE FACE OF INTIMACY

Intimacy, although often mistaken for sex, does not hinge on physical contact. Instead, it results from familiarity with another person's inner nature, such as their thoughts and feelings, which calls for trust and respect. Two or more people who feel safe enough to reveal their innermost selves have an opportunity to be intimate.

In the act of unmasking with others, you get to see yourself more clearly. According to Charlotte Kasl, PhD, author of *If the Buddha Dated*, a transformational book about relationships, this release of the true self leads to love. Speaking your truth—exposing the beautiful and the ugly, the talents and the deficiencies, the desires and the fears—dismantles your personal censor, freeing you to connect with others and take in the beauty of the moment. You become fully alive and vibrant.

Thus, intimacy brings us in closer contact with ourselves. And curiously, this practice in self-awareness cannot be undertaken alone. It requires you to reveal yourself to another while remaining open as they reveal themselves to you. Both you and the other person, while experiencing a deep connection, feel whole and complete as individuals. No one tries to fix the other. No one has to like what they hear. Acceptance of the other is unconditional, given with understanding, patience, and compassion. The moment feels tender and soothing, or energized and refreshing. Whether or not the outcome results in a long-term association, the experience of yourself in that flash of intimacy lasts forever.

Nor is intimacy shared only by lovers. You can seek levels of intimacy in *all* your relationships—with family, friends, business associates, even strangers. Although standards of behavior may apply in certain circumstances, the safer you feel to be who you are, the sooner you'll leap into joy. No longer harassed by worries and self-analysis, your mind can go wherever your heart wants to take it. Creativity flourishes. Ideas abound. Filled with energy, you'll spring into action. Why? Because intimacy unleashes the passion for living.

When the space between two people feels unsafe, on the other hand, energy is dissipated as each tries to figure out what to say and do to avoid being judged unfavorably. Driven by fear, some move into patterns of avoidance. Others draw battle lines, carefully strategizing how to change the "opponent." Or they surround themselves with walls of shame, blame, envy, and anger. In all three instances, negative thoughts can become so pervasive that the individuals numb themselves through addictions to television, the computer, drugs, sex, gambling, shopping, or working. They kill time. With it, they kill joy.

THE GREAT SABOTAGE

If intimacy is so joyful, why do we often avoid it? Because we are afraid of being hurt. After all, in revealing ourselves to others, we risk rejection, abandonment, betrayal, and a host of other painful emotions. Emotional injury goes deeper than injury to the physical body. What's more, whereas a physical wound tends to heal on its own, recovery from an emotional injury takes conscious effort on our part, and is best accomplished soon after the event. Yes, time can dull the pain. But leaving recuperation to the calendar is sure to result in protective scars rather than a regenerated spirit.

The more scarred-over our emotional wounds are, the fiercer is our desire to protect ourselves from intimacy. The mind jumps into hyperalert, scanning the horizon for the possibility of harm. Detecting even a faint likelihood of injury, it sends up bullet-proof walls. Consider, for example, the plot of the movie *When Harry Met Sally*. A man and woman who have been friends for years decide to date. Once sexual intimacy enters the picture, they distrust each other's motives. Pain from past relationships ultimately causes these two good friends to separate.

Other relationships die before they get started. One party claims, "You're the type of person who would want me to be a certain way; and then I'd feel trapped and guilty, and soon resent you and hate myself, so why bother," when what they mean is, "I'm afraid that I'd like you and you'd hurt me." Conversations in every new relationship—whether in the workplace, the local cafe, or the bedroom—resurrect old feelings of fear, disillusionment, humiliation, sacrifice, frustration, loss, or defeat. When self-awareness and disclosure do not play a role, the past dominates the present, causing prospective partners to flee from intimacy.

Most longer-lived relationships are no better off. A person who desperately needs to be loved will cling to their mate, taking on identities they believe are expected of them. Pouring energy into maintaining the facade, they refuse to allow themselves or their partner a shred of honest intimacy. They're afraid that if ever the mask drops, their partner will be disappointed. All the while, they experience a buildup of anger and resentment over not being loved for who they are, until one day the brew boils over. The pretender attacks mercilessly. The receiver either gets pummeled or fights back. Love doesn't stand a chance.

Even people who appear confident in a longtime relationship can harbor gremlins that raise walls of separation. Beautiful women who won't admit their age, doctors who become secretly disenchanted with their profession, and war veterans who refuse to speak of their military history will operate splendidly up to a point. But touch on a "hot spot" and they either shut down or affix themselves rigidly to an opinion. The door is shut on that particular room. No one is allowed inside, including themselves.

In the movie *Living Out Loud,* Judith, recently divorced, seeks desperately to find out who she is. When asked, "Did your husband leave you?" she replies, "*I* left me long before *he* did." The irony is that in relationship, where we are most able to come to know ourselves, we are most likely to lose ourselves.

Sometimes the detour sign is set by culture. In our society, for example, touching carries sexual innuendos. It's against company policy to touch one another at work. Friends are cautious about hugging and kissing. Physical contact has been relegated to the realms of mothers and lovers. Even then, touch is at times confused with power and control.

It's no wonder so many Westerners feel lonely, including those in committed relationships. Our fear of being hurt has sabotaged our happiness by keeping us at arm's length from the joys of love—the great connector.

RETURNING TO LOVE

Just as detaching from judgments, needs, and expectations promises rapture at work and at play, the same holds true in relationships.

Opening to love calls for letting go, over and over again. Whoever it is you are with, detaching from how you saw them in the past (even yesterday), from how you think they will behave in the present, and from your need to be loved will bring you soul to soul with who they are *right now*. After all, each day they are someone new—and so are you.

This moment-by-moment release will enable you to see others with fresh eyes. Yet it is not easy to accomplish. With friends, there is safety in relying on the outcome of conversations. There's security in predicting how much of yourself you can "be" with them, without suffering rejection. Yet staying in this mode with friends can keep you from growing.

With your lover, there's a reservoir of pleasant memories you may secretly yearn to re-create. While looking at your beloved, you may suddenly recall the magic of the first kiss you shared, the night you talked and laughed for hours, or your spontaneous acts of passion before the kids were born. But there's an inherent conflict of interest in saying "I love you" while imagining your partner behaving in a certain way. A partnership built on the subtle pact of "I'll be what you want if you'll be what I want" is equally compromised. When the pact is broken, you're apt to retreat in disappointment or stew with anger. Disappointment and anger, like fantasy, pull you away from the present moment.

Seeing with fresh eyes is just as challenging when meeting someone for the first time. Upon spotting a trait that reminds you of pain you've experienced with another person, you're likely to step into a suit of armor, turn defensive or combative, or put up walls of words or silence—anything to avoid letting them get too close. Or if meeting someone new triggers an early programming for compliance, you may end up seeing a movie you would never see on your own, succumbing to sex when you don't feel like it, smiling when you're unhappy, staying when you'd rather go, saying "yes" when your mind screams "no," or agreeing to less than acceptable treatment. In response, your body may tense up or your mind may turn to retaliation, leaving little room for the present to shine through.

Given the all-too-human propensity for wishful thinking, feelings of defeat, self-censuring, and acquiescence, how can you free your mind to float into the present moment with other people? By discovering them and recognizing who you are *at that moment* in relationship to them. Look "into" each person, gazing beyond their words to their fears, passions, and desires. At the same time, detach from your concerns and needs, clearing this clutter from the space you're sharing. If you feel jealous, you could say, "Oh, here I am, being jealous of my good friend for her achievements. I can feel jealous *and* still love her." Admit your disappointment over your boss's lack of acknowledgment without condemning him or calling him names. Instead of dashing off the first time your lover gets mad at you, uncover the reason for your impulse to run. Then love yourself in all your silly manifestations. In the stillness of detachment, you become a compassionate witness to your fears.

To be fully alive in relationships, break the bonds of past experiences. Cast aside your unmet expectations. Clear your mind and look each person in the eye. Then either decide to stay with the soul you see or determine that your soul's flame would burn brighter elsewhere.

Consciously choosing to exist in the moment requires a substantial dose of bravery, several dashes of perseverance, and practice in the art of discovery, especially in seeing like a poet and exercising beginner's mind (see chapter 8). Yet you can always start now. The next person you see, look them in the eye. Attempt to make a special connection, imagining that you may never have another opportunity to see them. Align your energy with your business partner's. Engage your colleagues at a heart level. Collaborate harmoniously with your neighbors. View your friends and family as new people each day, and delight in the transformations they're making. See your lover grow more beautiful every second. Notice the richness in every soul you meet.

Re-creating your relationships every day may threaten your sense of security. At the same time, it will liberate you to be yourself. Little in life is as exhilarating as finding there is nothing you should hide and then dropping your mask. Some people will accept the challenge to bare themselves with you; others will run. With those who join you in the vertical world, you'll experience the sweetness of being exactly who you are and feeling unconditionally loved.

Unmasking is always more potent than protecting yourself. In dropping your disguise, you can honor the being, the god, the "thou" in another—the greatest gift you can give. Simultaneously, you experience yourself as equally sacred, which is the highest privilege you can claim. When two brave naked souls come together, they form a conduit for rapture.

WEAVING "WHAT COULD BE" INTO "WHAT IS"

Seeing people with fresh eyes places you on the diving board. The leap comes with the words you speak and the emotions you willingly express. How do you create the space for these conversations to occur? What do you say? Speaking your truth is a spontaneous act. Even so, visioning what intimacy looks like generates a beam you can follow, much as the North Star provides direction to someone wandering in the desert.

While visioning, you will see your "possible self" unfolding in relationship with others. Then, as you go about your day, you will be able to test the waters, entering slowly enough to feel comfortable demonstrating the behaviors you've envisioned. To form open, honest, and joyful relationships through visioning, begin by brainstorming the qualities and behaviors likely to lead to an ideal relationship with all people, then specifically with friends, your partner, and your children. Finally, work with the exercise described in figure 11–1, on pages 212–213.

Your sample list of qualities and behaviors in each of the three categories might look something like this.

In all my relationships, I wish to:

- Resist the urge to give unwanted advice.
- Listen to objections and disagreements instead of planning an opposing argument.
- Become aware of my body's signals when I disagree, then look for the cause of my tightness, clenching, nervousness, or irregular breathing patterns.
- Detach from past memories that have produced grudges, resentment, and fear
- Calm my need to control.
- Accept—and never interrupt—a compliment.
- Remember that not getting what I want can be advantageous.
- Resist basing my self-worth on how I compare with others.

- Refuse to stereotype by race, gender, age, status, or looks.
- Reflect on what is separating my mind from my heart when I judge and criticize.
- Accept that some people won't like me—oh well.
- Conduct leave-taking with loving words. Think, "God be with you," as I say goodbye.
- Practice forgiving myself and others.
- Be fully present while conversing. Stay relaxed, communicate understanding, and respect their perceptions before expressing my own thoughts and feelings.
- Avoid below-the-belt attacks, whether stated directly or delivered indirectly in the form of sarcasm, lecturing, or teasing. Instead, speak honestly about what feels uncomfortable in the moment.
- Remember that everyone is on a path of their own.

When I'm with friends, I also wish to:
- Practice extreme forgiveness.
- Apologize quickly and sincerely after stepping on their toes.
- Remember that arguing can enhance understanding as long as it is directed at an issue, and not a person.
- Spend time together doing nothing.
- Tell the truth, soul to soul.
- Acknowledge that they are growing daily, and so am I.
- Love them deeply, whether or not they can receive my love or reciprocate.
- Acknowledge that at any time, the nature of a friendship may change. Rejoice in growth, even if in the moment it makes me sad.

When I'm with my lover or children, I also wish to:
- Value harmony over drama and chaos.
- Know that caring for them doesn't mean losing myself, my health, or my sense of well-being.
- Avoid criticizing, blaming, or running away when I feel hurt by them.
- Never pout or "suffer in silence."
- Refrain from manipulative ploys, such as teasing or baby-talk, when I'm uncomfortable stating my thoughts and feelings.

- Support them on their own paths, as opposed to those I've conjured up for them.
- Go on adventures together, experimenting with new places and activities.
- Avoid making them feel responsible for my happiness.
- Enjoy holding them.
- Look forward to seeing them.
- Allow them to enjoy slices of life without me.
- Commit to being present and in love no matter what.
- Have fun and laugh as often as possible.

If you decide to compile a separate list of qualities and behaviors to demonstrate with your lover, consider these two additional points. First, according to author and researcher Scott Silberman, both men and women name communication as the number one contributor to marital happiness. Each wants their mate to be a good friend, fully responsive and alive in the moment. Second, sex is rated as the number two gateway to joy. By combining number one with number two—physically consummating love with a fully open heart—you will experience one of life's most enchanting moments. Hence, you may want to start off your list with "Being a good friend" as the most important aspect of a relationship that includes a sexual connection.

Figure 11–1

A Vision of Love

To deepen the intimacy you feel with someone in your life, complete these steps.

- Identify the qualities and behaviors that would characterize your ideal interactions with this person.

- Write a few sentences describing this relationship in action.

- Now that you have a picture of your ideal relationship with this person, review it from time to time, to keep it fresh in your mind.

- If you have trouble bringing this picture to life, ask the other person if they, too, honor these qualities. Then, if there is agreement, you can together determine what it will take to make your vision real.

Your relationships may never fully match your pictures of them. But don't allow reality to spoil your dreams. Continue to weave your aspirations into the present moment, consciously moving in the direction of your visions. Many people will willingly join you in the moment. Then, too, someone who has experienced intimacy with you may one day retreat. If so, take heart. Remember that every encounter is a journey, rather than a destination—a flowing together, sometimes apart, hitting rocks, wallowing in stagnant pools, sometimes rushing, sometimes clinging, and sometimes lingering in the warmth of the contact. Stay open to the possibility of achieving each vision, with compassion and patience for yourself and for others.

COVISIONING YOUR RELATIONSHIPS

To increase the likelihood of deepening your relationships, try covisioning. Simply follow the procedure described in chapter 5: after completing your vision of how you'd like to be with your manager, coworkers, friends, family, and lover, ask each one to compose a picture of their own. Then one on one, with narratives in hand, discuss why you chose these images, underscore the parts most important to your happiness, and negotiate any points that conflict. By keeping the conversations judgment-free, you will have a good chance of integrating your visions into theirs, arriving in each case at a relationship you want to create together—a true covision.

Here's an example of a covisioned relationship, written by Gary and Darla as they approached their second wedding anniversary. Note that they divided their picture into categories—a technique that allows for easy reference as time passes.

Figure 11-2

Our Covision of Year Number Two

Teamwork

We are a team. We make decisions together, based on open dialogue and collaboration. Neither of us lets an issue go unaddressed if feelings are hurt. Business travel plans are announced as soon as possible, well before they are finalized. We commit to social engagements only after consulting each other. While out in public, we speak about each other with respect.

To refresh and renew, we vacation together for at least one week in winter and two weeks, separately or together, in summer. We celebrate each other's birthday and honor each other on different occasions as well.

Communication

No desire is too silly; no emotion is wrong; no subject matter taboo. We speak our minds as thoughts arise, delivering them thoughtfully and with respect. Our lifelong happiness together requires open and caring disclosures and acknowledgments. We show empathy and understanding, recognize each other's struggles, and share the pains and victories.

Private Time

Saturday mornings and afternoons are reserved for private time, which we spend on our own. By request, a weekday evening may also be reserved for private time. Such requests are not to be taken as rejections, but as acts of mental preservation.

Housekeeping

Although we employ a housekeeper, minor chores, such as making the bed, cleaning the counters, and emptying the garbage, are thoughtfully tended to as needed. We clean up after ourselves, do our personal laundry unless we choose to do our mate's, and cook for ourselves unless we decide to prepare a meal together. (Sunday dinners we cook in tandem.)

Weekends
Friday nights are up for grabs—if one of us wants to be with the other, we let it be known in advance. Saturdays are for individual projects or visiting with friends. Saturday nights and Sundays are spent together. On Sundays we shop, unless one of us would like to get the shopping out of the way earlier.

Reflection and Renewal
Although we strive for open, honest communication on a regular basis, we allocate one night during the last week of every month to discussing the state of our marriage. These conversations provide an opportunity to express unfulfilled desires and breaches of agreement before they start to fester. More importantly, we take this time to celebrate our relationship and our love for each other.

Six months after drafting their covision, Gary and Darla agreed that sticking to the teamwork and communication portions of their covision had been difficult. "The first month was easy, but then we slipped into old habits," Gary confessed. "Taking the time to reflect and to renew our commitment to the relationship really kept us on track."

What they enjoyed most about covisioning, they said, was aligning their expectations and defining boundaries that respect their individual needs. They agreed to repeat the process the following year.

Whether you are covisioning with your partner or with someone else in your life, remember to negotiate a win-win scenario free of sacrifice and denial. Also anticipate some modicum of personal loss—a debt paid to the spirit of creating something greater together. When your covision is complete, ensure that you and the other person agree wholeheartedly to the picture. If the energy is flowing freely *within* you, chances are that it will flow *between* you.

COMMITMENT
The final frontier to cross before entering the sphere of rapture in relationships is a *commitment to the quest*. Although you may deeply desire intimacy, those infamous imps known as power struggles, conflicts, and needs are sure to arise. In response, your doubts, fears, and anxieties

may jump at the chance to zip up your heart. And your self-preservation instincts may convince you to give up the quest and slip back into a passionless and barren comfort zone. Beware, however, of leading a guarded life. Those who protect themselves from hurt suffer most deeply from what they most dread—being alone.

The commitment to intimacy involves consciously choosing to "be in love" with a person exactly as they are in the moment. This task requires disciplined attention to your thoughts and feelings, and avoiding all escape hatches when conflicts erupt. "Forgoing love in the present out of anxiety about losing it in the future is a fool's bargain," writes Robert Gerzon, in his book *Finding Serenity in the Age of Anxiety.* To keep your heart open, renew your vow daily. Then any time you face troubled water, remind yourself that committing to love is the only way to stay afloat.

Once you've declared your commitment to a relationship, don't expect your partner to reciprocate. If they join you, all the better. If they don't, you have the choice to either continue to love them or leave.

Of course, committing to love calls for bravery. But if you don't take the risk, you're *sure* to lose. For instance, a forty-year-old client recently complained to me that he never married because he hasn't been able to "find the right person to commit to." Although matching values and interests is important when choosing a lifelong partner, commitment isn't about finding the ideal mate. It's about creating the ideal circumstances for love to bloom.

Many people associate commitment with imprisonment. The truth is that commitment to an intimate relationship is the essence of *freedom.* The boundaries defined by a commitment provide an open space for exploration. Without commitment, you are always wondering what is or isn't appropriate behavior, and what you can or cannot say and do. Yet when a friend, business associate, or lover commits to an open, honest relationship with you, you discover a playground on which to grow as human beings. You feel safe enough to express emotions. You may hurt at times; at other times, you'll feel ecstatic. When the heart tightens with fear, all it takes is a little reassurance to gently pry it open. Then as the relationship matures, you come to trust there will be celebrations to balance out disappointments.

Commitments don't have to include the word *forever.* But they should represent a willingness to be honest, alive, and present in all shared interactions for as long as the partnership exists, and to avoid seeking replacement partners when the going gets tough.

To practice commitment, begin with one person—preferably someone whom you trust will be sensitive to your opening heart. Then slowly reveal your thoughts, feelings, fears, and dreams. As soon as you realize that you can survive the experience, your anxiety will soften. Your mind will quiet down as you speak your truth.

Once you feel comfortable being intimate with this person, open your heart to another. Most people, upon sensing your sincerity, will welcome the opportunity to be real and honest with you. Why? Because most people want to find themselves while relating to others and to feel understood, respected, and loved. Honesty begets honesty. Giving love invites others to love us. We all seek the freedom to be who we are in the company of others.

Continuing on, one person at a time, you'll soon develop unconditional honesty and a heightened awareness of the colors, smells, sounds, tastes, and delicacies of life. You'll notice how another person breathes while speaking, see the bright green plaid on his new shirt, smell her latest shampoo, observe the nervousness in his fingers, catch the enthusiasm in her eyes. As you become more visible to others, the entire world becomes more visible to you. You stand vibrantly alive, centered squarely in the vertical world.

Yet don't just give love. Accept it, as well. When heart energy flows in both directions, you merge with the moment. Its light then penetrates all barriers—easing anger, soothing pain, and relieving loneliness. The circle of energy established between you, as two open-hearted people, transforms each of you in ways you could never achieve on your own.

Ultimately, the intimacy of jumping into life with another is the essence of spirituality. According to Zen master Osho, in "being with" others, as opposed to "thinking with" others, you no longer speculate. You participate. As your sense of separateness fades, you begin to feel at home wherever you are. You accept that you're an essential piece of the puzzle called life. Then you settle into your rightful place in the universe, feeling love falling on you from all dimensions.

Intimacy is nourishing. When you initiate it, you contribute something precious to the whole of humankind. Is this not the greatest life purpose there could be? Surely, as my massage therapist said, learning to be whole within our relationships is how we come to know the honor of being human.

CHAPTER 12

Waking Up
with Joy

This is the precious present.

—Timothy Miller

I was speaking on the phone with a client who was struggling with a career decision. Although she felt stagnant in her position and disrespected by management, she was afraid to leave, fearful of a decrease in both her professional status and her income. Shifting the conversation away from pros and cons, I asked her: "What makes you happy? What makes your heart glow? What sing-along song, tantalizing smell, magnificent sight, gutsy act, pleasant surprise, friendly voice, sinful taste, and private space evokes a smile?"

The first words out of her mouth were, "Nothing. I work all day. I'm too stressed to do anything but bathe and sleep."

I pressed her, looking for the faintest ray of delight.

She finally caved in. Within minutes, she was giggling about seeing her boss get hit in the butt by a computer cart and about eating a scrumptious brownie for lunch.

Interrupting her revelry, I asked, "Steph, what's your next step?"

"Out," she said.

Detached at last from the fear, Stephanie knew that her passion lay beyond the walls of her current place of employment. When she stood in the light of her joy, there was no deliberation—only forward motion in a direction that would better serve her purpose.

Our conversation reminded me of Bill Mayer's comment in his book *The Magic in Asking the Right Questions*, where he notes, "If at first you don't succeed, then ask yourself better questions." The solution to dilemmas, he reminds us, can often be found by shifting from analyzing the problem to uncovering buried dreams and desires. As in Stephanie's case, many times the question is not "Should I go?" but rather "How can I grow?" Still, it takes an uncluttered mind and an unwavering trust to arrive at an honest answer.

We spent the last ten minutes of the call talking about how simple life can be when we recognize how rich we are regardless of external circumstances. As soon as the mind clears, the answers emerge. And as we bravely act on them, our lives transform.

After hanging up the receiver, I thanked God for my clients and a profession that keeps me focused on what it's like to live in abundance and faith. I'm not there every minute of every day. Nor is my life exempt from disappointment and fear. But I know that if I slip, if I begin trudging or frantically running through the horizontal world, I can always find the door back to "now."

You, too, can deliberately step into the present. Already, you probably suspect that today is not just a block of time to be endured until a better tomorrow creeps over the horizon. And knowing *who you really are* and *what you want to create*, you no doubt realize that the moment, even if it contains disappointment and shattered dreams, holds seeds of joy.

To keep this knowledge alive within you, recommit yourself daily to the path of joy. Stand for what you believe in. Hold on, despite people who question your sanity about refusing a job offer or ending a friendship that was based more on outer dictates than inner ones. Sing over dirty diapers, mangled faxes, snarled traffic, burnt dinners, and leaky roofs. Crank up the volume to drown out judgment and gossip.

In short, become a spiritual warrior. Eugene Peterson, author of *Leap Over a Wall*, says, "We must live largely, aware of grace and beauty in every detail." Peterson invites us to carry on like the biblical hero David, whose life was riddled with sibling rivalry, murder, adultery, humiliation, false pride, rejection, and revenge. By living fully in the moment, with passion, faith, and love, David, despite the hardships, came to know God.

Every morning, declare that your life matters. Inspect your personal foundation and fill in the cracks. Recall your purpose, set your sights on your vision, and prepare to hold fast to what you value in the face of ridicule, criticism, and self-doubt. As the queen in *Alice's Adventures in Wonderland* advises, "Believe in six impossible things before breakfast." If you feel your joy each day, you will program yourself to believe in its power.

In his short story, "Strange Wine," Harlan Ellison wrote about a man who, while strolling on the beach near his home, was so depressed about the state of his business, his marriage, and his family that he walked into the ocean and quickly drowned. The next thing he knew, he was lying in a sea of sand. Not so much as a blade of grass disrupted the barren landscape. Suddenly, an army of giant crabs appeared over the crest of a nearby sand dune and ran toward him. He tried to escape but could not, for his legs were shaped like a crab's. The army quickly surrounded him.

"What was it like?" one crab asked him. The others echoed, "What was it like?"

"What was *what* like?" he replied.

"Your life!"

"What are you talking about?"

"Earth. Your life on earth. You were given a lifetime on the pleasure planet, the one called earth, as a reward for living ten exemplary lives here."

The man looked back on his most recent life: on the woman he married, whom he still thought of as lovely despite their problems; on the business successes that outweighed the difficulties; on the strong-willed and handsome children he raised; and on the beautiful home he left behind when he walked into the ocean. He realized he had been given a rare gift indeed—a few precious years in the corner of the universe most filled with light.

The story concludes, "He remembered the rain and the feel of the beach sand beneath his feet, and the ocean rolling in to whisper its eternal song, and on just such nights as those he had despised on earth, he slept and dreamed good dreams...of life on the pleasure planet."

You are more fortunate. Waking up to see that you are actually living on the pleasure planet is an available choice. You can let disappointment contaminate your relationships and poison you to the point of anger, illness, and depression. Or you can regard difficulties as stepping stones toward change and growth—toward letting loving friends, flitting hummingbirds, and a mud-pie gift from the boy next door renew your understanding of what's most important.

While journeying into the vertical world, you will have many opportunities from sunrise to sunset each day to decide if you'll greet the next morning in misery or in joy. To help make the most pleasurable choice, plant seeds of gratitude, abundance, and laughter. Then water them daily.

SPEAK YOUR GRATITUDE

I have found that the most immediate way to center myself in the present is to stop and say "thank you" for my life. While in line at the grocery store, I'm grateful I can afford Starbucks ice cream. In traffic jams, I'm grateful that my car doesn't overheat and that Phoenix has a good classical music radio station. When I think of skipping my morning workout, I remind myself of how lucky I am to be strong and limber. When I wish my neighbor would go home, I say my grace for living next to someone I can trust to care for my house when I leave town. When I feel discouraged, I remember that not getting what I want has at times been a stroke of luck, leading to something better. Gratitude gives me faith that my path is unfolding perfectly, even when events test my patience and my tolerance.

As you plant and tend your seeds of gratitude, people may roll their eyes at you or call you Pollyanna—an early-twentieth-century heroine in a novel by Eleanor Porter—whose name has come to signify irrepressible, and sometimes obnoxious optimism. But don't let the criticism ruffle your feathers. The truth is, becoming more Pollyannaish will help you stay centered in the pleasures of the present.

Pollyanna kept her spirits up by playing the glad game, cheerfully naming all the things that made her happy. Julie Andrews, in the movie *The Sound of Music*, sang of a similar strategy: "When the dog bites, when the bees sting, when I'm feeling sad, I simply remember my favorite things, and then I don't feel so bad." Instructions for playing an updated version of the glad game are given in figure 12–1.

There is a Zen story about a man who, while running from a lion, fell off a cliff. Grabbing hold of a tree branch on the way down, he was

---

FIGURE 12—1

The Glad Game

Instead of resigning yourself to misery, redesign your thoughts by naming your favorite things. Follow the steps below.

- List a variety of things you are grateful for. Here are some possibilities:

Pictures in the cookbook	Unexpected hugs
My favorite chair	Fresh juice
No line at the post office	Time for a bath
A friend who woke me to say good night	Throwing out junk mail without reading it
Falling in love	The smell of freshly cut grass
Standing naked in the kitchen	On-time airline flights
Real mayonnaise	Microwave ovens
The $20 bill I found in my coat pocket	E-mail from a friend I haven't seen in years
Old Levi's that fit again	A good haircut
A considerate car mechanic	Freshly washed sheets
Traffic going the other way	The full moon on a clear summer night

- Read your list aloud on days when your boss is crabby, your child is mean to you, or your health takes a turn for the worst.

- Every day, look for one new item to add to your list. The search alone will brighten your perspective.

---

able to stop his fall. When he looked up, he saw the lion waiting for him at the top of the cliff. At that moment, the branch started to crack. When the man looked down, he saw a hungry bear waiting for him on the ground far below. Instead of collapsing in fear, he looked straight at the mountain wall, where a patch of red protruded from a crack in the granite. "Ah, fresh strawberries," said the man. He savored the fruit as the branch broke, sending him to his doom.

When beset by threats from every direction, you need not tremble in fear of what might happen. Instead, focus on what is in front of you. Life unfolds. You can either fill it with worry and regret or savor it with gratitude. Your experience of life is up to you.

FEEL ABUNDANT

The second seed to plant on your journey into the vertical world is a feeling of abundance, based on the belief that everything you want is readily available. When asked where the money would come from to fund a huge project, author and spiritual teacher Deepak Chopra answered, "From where it is right now." He knew the world was filled with plenty of everything he needed.

When we are afraid of not having enough money, love, or recognition in our lives, we become jealous, judgmental, and victimized. While focusing on what we don't have, we feel small, constricted, and inadequate. As soon as we shift into knowing that everything we seek is available, we feel large, generous, and worthy. Love flows. We attract what we need.

Abundance encompasses all of life's riches. To *feel* abundant, however, you must know which riches you seek. "I believe that the very purpose of our life is to seek happiness," says the Dalai Lama in *The Art of Happiness*. The happiness he speaks of refers not so much to items we can own as to the less tangible *quality of life*. With this in mind, try asking yourself, "What brings me happiness?"

Look around you. Which of the items in your world enhance your quality of life? Your car, your kitchen gadgets, the softness of your bed? Now go deeper. What soothes your anxiety when you come home from work? Your mate, soft music, the all-knowing cat that curls up in your lap? Do you have a favorite outdoor sitting spot where you can just be a "nobody" for an hour? How about a special book that draws you into a delectable universe? Go deeper yet. Think of the people, animals, plant life, sounds, tastes, and smells that comfort you. What else brings a smile to your heart—a child to read to, or a group of friends to play cards or discuss the meaning of life with? What do you love about your work? What else do you do that stirs your passion?

Once you have defined your sources of happiness, ask yourself if there is anything more you need before you can declare yourself "rich." If it turns out that something is needed, trust that it is waiting for you to find it. In such instances, open yourself to the possibility that it is within your reach. Then wake up every day knowing you are that much closer to your dreams.

Most likely, you will find that abundance is not a physical condition after all. It's an emotional state, and it's always available to you. You cannot see it or hold it. You can only sense that, in terms of your quality of life, you are fabulously wealthy.

LIBERATE YOUR LAUGHTER

Essayist and poet Ralph Waldo Emerson wrote, "For every minute you are angry, you lose sixty seconds of happiness." Research indicates the loss is even greater. When flooded with emotions such as rage, hate, blame, and depression, the body releases toxic chemicals that deplete the immune system, contributing to serious illness. Simultaneously, the energy these emotions generate is released from the body, plaguing communications and relationships. Over time, such emotions destroy optimism, leaving a breeding ground for lethargy, passivity, and a horde of addictions. Whether expressed or suppressed, your emotions shape your life—far more than your thoughts do. Trying to modify your thoughts without altering the underlying emotions is a lesson in futility, and is the reason affirmations alone do not change lives.

The best way to fortify your immunity to anger, depression, and apathy is by planting seeds of laughter—or better yet, laughing outright. However, if you're already in the throes of negativity, you might find it hard to so much as giggle. In such instances, a cleansing may be needed to clear your emotional drain pipes and make way for lighter feelings.

To cleanse, begin by acknowledging that you have emotional

blockages. Signs include digestive problems (the body instinctively stops breaking down food to prepare for a fear-provoking encounter), petty arguments, vengeful fantasies, uncontrollable crying, complaints of persecution, images of yourself as a rescuer (which condones victimization and powerlessness, and helps you avoid dealing with your own emotions), indifference, addictions, and a desire to dodge another miserable day. Or maybe you're too busy to wash your face at night, too rushed to fasten your seat belt, and too distracted to listen to a friend. How can you find joy when you can't even find time to floss your teeth?

Next, begin a physical cleansing. Andrew Weil, MD, recommends this treatment for depression: exercise for at least thirty minutes five days a week, meditate, relax, stop drinking alcohol, refuse all sedatives including antihistamines, steer clear of sugar, eat more fruits and vegetables, and get a weekly massage. In response, clots of melancholy will loosen and wash away.

In purging your body, you remove the armor protecting your feelings. If pain, sorrow, and anger spew forth, don't stop the flow. You've masked, minimized, blamed, and cradled these feelings long enough. It's time to acknowledge them, work through them, and get on with living. If you feel overwhelmed by the outpouring of agonizing emotions, seek the assistance of a licensed counselor or therapist to help you understand your pain.

Medication is ill-advised unless you've received a medical diagnosis, such as a chemical imbalance, that must be pharmaceutically corrected. Author and spiritual minister Marianne Williamson tells the story of a woman who claimed that if she gave up her antidepressants, she would go to bed and cry for days. Williamson said, "Perfect. Go cry for three days. Then on the fourth, get up." She adds, "Millions are on antidepressants, including over half of the adult female population. No pain, loss, or rejection is worse than being disconnected from yourself. God cannot enter that which you deny."

A newspaper article that reported the death of John F. Kennedy Jr. quoted a friend as saying, "This family continues very strong. I admire their strength. I haven't seen a tear yet, and that's beautiful." Kennedy's friend, like many antidepressant advocates, actually believes that stuffing grief is a virtue. In reality, quite the opposite is true.

For this reason, it may be wise to *push* yourself to feel your emotions. Cry, grieve, scream them out. Walk with them. Breathe them. Partner with them. Speak to them as if they were housemates who must now leave. In feeling your suffering, you can come to understand why such emotions exist. You can name the fears and needs underlying your pain. With this awareness of your emotions comes the power to be free of their tyranny.

Even if you have a medically diagnosed condition that requires pharmaceutical treatment, you can find greater pleasure. Try clearing your body of other toxins and exploring your fears and needs with a therapist. Joy isn't biased; it's available to everyone.

This work is not easy. Yet it is well worth the courage you give it. The more you stay present to the moment as you acknowledge your accumulated bitterness, loneliness, and sadness, the sooner the light of compassion and love will shine through from your heart.

Here's more good news. Soon after beginning your cleansing, you will have at your disposal the most powerful weapon there is against relapse—a sense of humor. Laughter heightens serotonin levels, decreasing the urge to deny painful feelings or to numb them through medication. Laughter provides physiological healing as well, which can further bolster you against relapse. In essence, seeing the funny side of everyday situations turns drudgery into amusement. So develop an eye for whimsy. See the silliness in human behavior. Listen with a playful ear. The world is brimming with fodder for big laughs.

Comedian Steve Allen, in his aptly titled book *How to Be Funny*, says that being funny depends on *attitude*. You have to know you've got a funny side and be willing to hunt for humor wherever you go. "Brainwash yourself with as much humor as possible," writes Allen. "If you make a habit to listen to comedy albums, see comedy films, and frequent comedy clubs, you will inevitably become a bit funnier, in precisely the same way that you would become a better bridge player if you immersed yourself in the company and culture of those to whom the game of bridge is enormously important." Read funny books. Hang out with funny people. Eventually, Allen says, you'll become a magnet for funniness. Humor will find you. It's not that funnier things will happen to you than to others, but rather that your sensitivity to comedy will enable you to see the humor that they might miss.

A further aid for brightening up comes from burn victims, who are taught to ease their pain by going to their "laughing place." Whereas most burn victims learn this technique in the midst of a crisis, you can prepare in advance by working with the exercise described in figure 12–2.

FIGURE 12–2

Go to Your Laughing Place

To prevent paralysis and fear from setting in after a crisis, lay the groundwork now by completing these steps.

- Find at least 3 stories, songs, or pictures that make you laugh when you think of them.
- Jot down the highlights of the stories, write out the words of the songs, or cut out the pictures. Then store these pages in a spot where you can refresh your memory of their contents at least once a month. (Update them with new material as time goes on.)
- Whenever you need to jolt yourself out of emotional or physical pain, go to your laughing place by recalling one or more of these ticklers.

We all have hearts that break, bodies that age, friends who betray us, and minds that breed shame. The door to all that you envision opens wide when, having felt your suffering, you quickly return to the joy of living. And for that, laughter is your secret key.

LEAP!

How you wake up each morning sets the tone for a good part of your day. Wake up eager to create something new, or thankful to watch the sun spread its light over the nearby treetops, or simply to be all of who you are. And there you'll stand—at the threshold of the vertical world.

But what if you wake up resistant to the day, or fearful of the unknowns that lurk in its crevices? This morning, for example, I couldn't get out of bed. The roar of a car engine invaded the quiet. I heard the newspaper land in the driveway. My cat chastised me for neglecting to feed her breakfast. I rolled over. The digital numbers on the clock glared at me, mocking my delay.

Finally, I dragged myself out of bed and began to write. While struggling to set words to paper, I realized I was afraid to end this chapter. After shutting off the computer, I'd be ready to put the book out into the world. Would people like it? Will anyone care about what I have to say?

So it is with life. We can choose the safe road, where the risks are few—as are the challenges and passions. Or we can go after our dreams, exposing ourselves to possible rejection, judgment, and disappointment. Acting on this choice requires courage. Can you speak your truth, knowing that the freedom it will grant is more powerful than fears of ridicule and condemnation? Can you commit to giving 100 percent, knowing that although you will be standing naked to the world, you will never have this day to do over again?

If you answer "yes" to these questions, then all you need to do every morning is take a deep breath and *choose* to get up. Recognize what was taunting you and laugh out loud. Then jump up and down on your mattress and leap into the glorious day.

Resources

BOOKS

Joy of Life

Allen, Steve. *How to Be Funny: Discovering the Comic You*. Columbus, OH: Prometheus, 1998.

Aronie, Nancy Slonim. *Writing from the Heart: Tapping the Power of Your Inner Voice*. New York: Hyperion, 1998.

Breathnach, Sarah Ban. *Simple Abundance: A Daybook of Comfort and Joy*. New York: Warner Books, 1995.

Breathnach, Sarah Ban. *Something More: Excavating Your Authentic Self*. New York: Warner Books, 1998.

Brodie, Richard. *Virus of the Mind*. Seattle, WA: Integral Press, 1995.

Buechner, Frederick. *The Longing for Home*. San Francisco: Harper, 1997.

Childre, Doc Lew, Howard Martin, and Donna Beech. *The HeartMath Solution: The HeartMath Institute's Revolutionary Program for Engaging the Power of the Heart's Intelligence*. New York: Harper Collins, 1999.

Chopra, Krishan. *Your Life Is in Your Hands: The Path to Lasting Health and Happiness*. Boston: Element Books, 1997.

Crisp, Wendy Reid. *Do As I Say, Not As I Did*. New York: Perigee, 1997.

The Dalai Lama and Howard Cutler, MD. *The Art of Happiness: A Handbook for Living*. New York: Riverhead, 1999.

deAngelis, Barbara. *Real Moments*. New York: Delacorte, 1994.

Fortgang, Laura Berman. *Take Yourself to the Top*. New York: Warner Books, 1998.

Gawain, Shakti. *Creating True Prosperity*. Novato, CA: New World Library, 1996.

Hoff, Benjamin. *The Tao of Pooh*. New York: E. P. Dutton, 1982.

Leonard, Thomas. *The Portable Coach: 28 Surefire Strategies for Business and Personal Success*. New York: Scribner, 1998.

Mayer, Bill. *The Magic in Asking the Right Questions*. Chicago: Mayer Press, 1997.

McKay, Matthew, Martha Davis, and Patrick Fanning. *Thoughts & Feelings: Taking Control of Your Moods and Your Life*. Oakland, CA: New Harbinger, 1997.

Minchinton, Jerry. *Maximum Self-Esteem: The Handbook for Reclaiming Your Sense of Self-Worth*. Vanzant, MO: Arnford Corporation, 1993.

Myers, David, PhD. *The Pursuit of Happiness: Discovering the Pathway to Fulfillment, Well-Being and Enduring Personal Joy*. New York: Avon, 1993.

Richardson, Cheryl. *Take Time for Your Life: A Personal Coach's 7-Step Program for Creating the Life You Want*. New York: Broadway Books, 1998.

Sapolsky, Robert M. *Why Zebras Don't Get Ulcers: An Updated Guide to Stress, Stress-Related Diseases, and Coping*. New York: W. H. Freeman and Company, 1994.

Sinatra, Stephen, MD. *Optimum Health*. New York: Bantam Books, 1996.

Somer, Elizabeth. *Age-Proof Your Body: Your Complete Guide to Lifelong Vitality*. New York: Morrow and Company, 1998.

Vanzant, Iyanla. *One Day My Soul Just Opened Up: 40 Days and 40 Nights towards Spiritual Strength and Personal Growth*. New York: Simon & Schuster, 1998.

Weeks, Dr. David, and Jamie James. *Secrets of the Super-Young*. New York: Villard Books, 1998.

Weil, Andrew, MD. *8 Weeks to Optimum Health: A Proven Program for Taking Full Advantage of Your Body's Natural Healing Power*. New York: Knopf, 1997.

Wieder, Marcia. *Doing Less and Having More*. New York: William Morrow and Co., 1998.

Zukav, Gary. *The Seat of the Soul*. New York: Simon & Schuster, 1999.

Meaningful Work

Barrett, Richard. *A Guide to Liberating Your Soul*. Waynesville, NC: Fulfilling Books, 1995.

Blum, Arlene. *Annapurna: A Woman's Place*. San Francisco: Sierra Club, 1980.

Csikszentmihalyi, Mihaly. *Flow: Psychology of Optimal Experience*. New York: Harper & Row, 1990.

Goleman, Daniel. *Emotional Intelligence*. New York: Bantam Books, 1995.

Goss, Tracy. *The Last Word on Power*. New York: Doubleday, 1996.

Hendricks, Gay, and Kate Ludeman. *The Corporate Mystic: A Guidebook for Visionaries with Their Feet on the Ground*. New York: Bantam Books, 1996.

Murphy, Michael, and Rhea A. White. *In the Zone: The Transcendent Experience in Sports*. Reading, MA: Addison-Wesley, 1978.

Sher, Barbara. *Wishcraft: How to Get What You Really Want*. New York: Viking, 1979.

Towery, Twyman L. *The Wisdom of Wolves: Principles for Creating Personal Success and Professional Triumphs*. Naperville, IL: Sourcebooks Inc., 1997.

Whyte, David. *The Heart Aroused: Poetry and the Preservation of the Soul in Corporate America.* New York: Doubleday, 1994.

Whyte, David. *The House of Belonging: Poems.* Langley, WA: Many Rivers Press, 1996.

Joyful Relationships

Buber, Martin, trans. Walter Kaufmann. *I and Thou.* New York: Charles Scribner's Sons, 1970.

Chopra, Deepak, MD. *The Path to Love.* New York: Harmony Books, 1997.

Gerzon, Robert. *Finding Serenity in the Age of Anxiety.* New York: Macmillan Publishing, 1997.

Kasl, Charlotte, PhD. *If the Buddha Dated: A Handbook for Finding Love on a Spiritual Path.* New York: Penguin Books, 1999.

Mitchell, Tamara and Wayne. *Your Other Half.* Springfield, MO: Echo Work Publishers, 1998.

Ornish, Dean, MD. *Love and Survival.* New York: HarperCollins, 1998.

Pearce, Joseph Chilton. *Magical Child.* New York: Plume, 1992.

Savage, Elayne, PhD. *Don't Take It Personally!* Oakland, CA: New Harbinger, 1997.

Sherven, Judith, and James Sniechowski. *The New Intimacy.* Deerfield Beach, FL: Health Communications, 1997.

Sills, Judith, PhD. *Excess Baggage: Getting Out of Your Way.* New York: Viking Penguin, 1993.

Waldman, Mark Robert. *The Art of Staying Together: Embracing Love, Intimacy, and Spirit in Relationships.* Los Angeles: J. P Tarcher, 1998.

Spirituality

Buechner, Frederick. *The Magnificent Defeat.* San Francisco: Harper, 1966.

Campbell, Joseph, with Bill Moyers. *The Power of Myth*. New York: Doubleday, 1988.

Frankl, Victor. *Man's Search for Meaning*. Boston: Beacon Press, 1959.

Gibran, Kahlil. *The Vision: Reflections on the Way of the Soul*. New York: Penguin, 1998.

Kushner, Lawrence. *God Was in This Place and I, i Did Not Know*. Woodstock, VT: Jewish Lights Publishing, 1991.

Miller, Timothy. *How to Have What You Want: Discovering the Magic and Grandeur of Ordinary Existence*. New York: Henry Holt, 1995.

Peterson, Eugene. *Leap Over a Wall: Earthy Spirituality for Everyday Christians*. New York: HarperCollins, 1997.

Reps, Paul, and Nyogen Senzaki. *Zen Flesh, Zen Bones*. Boston: Charles E. Tuttle, 1957.

Williamson, Marianne. *A Woman's Worth*. New York: Random House, 1993.

MAGAZINES

Fast Company
800-688-1545
www.fastcompany.com

Going Bonkers
800-403-8850
www.goingbonkers.com

IMPROVISATION ACTING CLASSES

Artistic New Directions
212-875-1857
ArtNewDir@aol.com
www.improv.net

In Los Angeles—Gary Austin
800-DOGTOES
wkshopinfo@aol.com

In New York—Carol Fox Prescott
CFPrescott@aol.com

ASSESSMENT SOURCES

Coach University
800-48-COACH
www.coachu.com

TTI Performance Systems
800-869-6908
www.ttidisc.com

COACHING REFERRAL SERVICES

International Coach Federation
888-ICF-3131
www.coachfederation.org

Coach University
800-48-COACH
www.coachu.com
www.coachreferral.com

Coaches Training Institute
800-691-6008
www.thecoaches.com

E-MAIL NEWSLETTERS

Daily Coaching Tip
Sponsored by Coach University
coachingtips-on@lists.dailycast.com

The Innovative Professional's (TIP's) Letter
Published by Philip Humbert
www.philiphumbert.com

Practical Psychology
Published by Lloyd J. Thomas, PhD
Practical Psychology-On@lists.webvalance.com

Take Time for Your Life
Published by Cheryl Richardson
subscribe@cherylrichardson.com

About the Author

Marcia Reynolds is a master at attracting bright new chapters into her life. After turning twenty years old in jail, she chose freedom and completed her college degree, graduating summa cum laude. From there, she earned two master's degrees, moved up the corporate ladder to the top rungs, then left to start Covisioning, a coaching and leadership training organization. In 1999, she was elected president of the International Coach Federation. She is also active with the National Speakers Association and on the board of Southwest Behavioral Health.

In her role as principal of Covisioning, Marcia provides executive coaching, strategic planning, leadership and personal effectiveness training, and team-weaving workshops. Clients range from individuals to a diverse blend of corporations and organizations including high-tech firms, health-care corporations, state and federal agencies, and not-for-profit groups. Classes are delivered in Asia and Europe, as well as throughout the Americas.

Marcia also presents keynotes and workshops internationally on the power of presence, emotional intelligence, and the art of coaching. She is the author of two audiocassette programs, *Being in the Zone: The Secrets of Performance Excellence* and *Golf in the Zone: How to Master the Mental Game of Golf*. Her work has been featured in *Health Magazine*, *The New York Times*, and the *New England Financial Times*, and she has appeared on radio and television talk shows and news programs both here and abroad. Although she has traveled the world for both pleasure and work, Marcia continues to live where she was born and raised—in sunny Phoenix, Arizona.

Order Form

Quantity	Amount
_____ *Capture the Rapture: How to Step Out of Your Head and Leap into Life* ($16.95)	_____
Sales tax of $1.05 per book for Arizona residents	_____
Shipping & handling ($4.00 for first book; $1.00 for each additional book)	_____
Total amount enclosed	_____

Please allow 2–3 weeks for shipping.
Quantity discounts available.

Method of payment

❐ Check or money order enclosed (made payable to **Covisioning** in US currency only)

❐ MasterCard   ❐ American Express   ❐ VISA   ❐ Discover

Card number: _____ Exp. date: _____

Signature: _____

Please contact your local bookstore or mail your order, together with your name, address, and check, money order, or charge-card information, to:

Hathor Hill Press
PO Box 5012, Scottsdale, AZ 85261

Phone toll-free: 888-998-5064   Fax: 602-553-3791
E-mail orders: Orders@Covisioning.com
E-mail correspondence: Marcia@Covisioning.com
Web site: www.covisioning.com